A delicious exploration of the Jewish holidays, with illuminating conversations and meals shared by friends: a rabbi and a cook.

For many of the Jewish Diaspora, experiencing the holidays might mean lighting a menorah for Chanukah, or hosting a Passover seder. But, if celebrated with an understanding of the storied customs behind the festivities, these occasions can be so much more than candles and matza. Following the lunisolar calendar, James Beard Award–winning author Susan Simon and Rabbi Zoe B Zak devote chapters to fourteen unique holidays. From Selichot to Rosh HaShanah, Purim to Pesach, every holiday has its own history, interpretation, and foods, with seasonal kosher recipes that reimagine traditional dishes from the entire Diaspora population with flair.

More than a cookbook, *The Cook and the Rabbi* is a testament to the resilient versatility of the Jewish people and their traditions. With Zoe's thoughtful insights and Susan's appealing recipes, there's no end to the ways you might celebrate the holidays and make your personal relationship with them uplifting, inspiring, and deeply fulfilling. *Chag Sameach*!

THE COOK
and
THE RABBI

THE COOK and THE RABBI

**Recipes and Stories
to Celebrate
the Jewish Holidays**

**SUSAN SIMON
AND ZOE B ZAK**

ART BY SUSAN SIMON

Countryman Press

An Imprint of W. W. Norton & Company
Celebrating a Century of Independent Publishing

For information about special discounts for bulk purchases, please contact
W. W. Norton Special Sales at specialsales@wwnorton.com or 800-233-4830

Manufacturing through Imago
Book design by Allison Chi

Countryman Press
www.countrymanpress.com

An imprint of W. W. Norton & Company, Inc.
500 Fifth Avenue, New York, NY 10110
www.wwnorton.com

978-1-68268-810-6

10 9 8 7 6 5 4 3 2 1

HEBREW MONTHS

NISSAN	~	march – april
IYAR	~	april – may
SIVAN	~	may – june
TAMMUZ	~	june – july
AV	~	july – august
ELUL	~	august – september
TISHREI	~	september – october
HESHVAN	~	october – november
KISLEV	~	november – december
TEVET	~	december – january
SHEVAT	~	january – february
ADAR	~	february – march

Contents

Introduction

Susan Simon—The Cook

As long as I've been aware that I am Jewish, I've been quietly proud and happy to identify with the ancient religion. I grew up in a secular home where there was little to no attempt to recognize our religion in a formal way. But neither was there an effort to deny our deeply heroic descendants and what they had endured over centuries to keep Judaism alive, relevant, and thriving.

The small Connecticut city where I grew up was a short train ride away from New York City, which made it possible for me to satisfy my ever-since-I-can-remember yearning to travel, to explore and to experience new things with a few trips into the metropolis, tour museums, or see a Broadway show. Short summer vacations to Nantucket, after my mother read *Moby Dick* (and an eventual yearslong residency there), kept me stable until I devised a plan to leave Bard College before I graduated and begin a real journey to a few exciting spots in the world: Italy for eight years, the Seychelles Islands for a year, Morocco for a few months, all the while checking out anything Jewish: the Moorish revival Tempio Maggiore in Florence; the Mellah, the Jewish quarter in Marrakech; the great Jewish neighborhood in the Marais area of Paris; and so on. Then, I moved to the überexciting spot of my childhood, New York City. That move sparked an interest, not exactly in Judaism as a religious practice, but in the holidays. If you live in New York or have visited it during Jewish holidays it's easy to find the joy, or sometimes sorrow, in the ubiquitous, citywide celebrations.

Holidays, if celebrated with some of the long histories and customs attached to the festivities, have a clever way of sneaking more than food, music, and costumes into your psyche.

After longtime New York City residence, I moved about 100 miles north of it to a town that shares the name of the mighty river that spills out into the Atlantic Ocean at the city's bottom, Hudson. I was holding on to holiday thoughts when I first experienced a celebration at Temple Israel of Catskill and listened to the gorgeous voice of Rabbi Zoe B Zak intoning Kol Nidre, the chant that begins the fast of Yom Kippur. My friend and agent Charlotte Sheedy was with me during that first service. When it was over and we gathered our stunned selves back together, Charlotte said, "We have to meet the rabbi." We did, with an idea for a book. This one.

My background is food—and the visual arts. I'm inspired by food, both its flavor and physical beauty, and its place—whether its origins in history, its seasonality, or simply a puzzle that I've completed with all gathered information. Food has a story to tell.

With the recipes (and artwork) in this book, I aim to tell you some stories with each recipe and why I've chosen them. The recipes are influenced by the dishes prepared by the populations of the Jewish Diaspora who prepared food like that of their neighbors—while keeping to kosher dietary law (only mammals that chew their cuds and have cloven hooves, seafood must have fins and scales, meat and dairy can't be eaten together)—whether in Kerala, South India; Addis Ababa, Ethiopia; Porto, Portugal; Thessaloniki, Greece; or right here in the Hudson Valley where ingredient seasonality and my own creative impulses are the greatest muses.

I'm aware that, for most people, holidays mean a return to the same food, decorations, faces, and conversations that haven't been with us since the last time we gathered together for a celebration. There's a sense of expectation that comes along with planning a holiday meal. What to make, who'll contribute, and how to supplement the table.

If you're Jewish and already have an expected plan that works for you—for example, on Rosh HaShanah, Chanukah, and Passover, you may choose a beef brisket, roast chicken, potato latkes, or matza ball soup—I ask you to please step out of your comfort zone, take a leap of faith, and add something new to your menu from the choices offered on the pages of this book, such as Spicy, Sweet, and Sour Braised Venison (page 76) with pomegranate molasses, Roast Chicken with Apricot Butter-Maple Syrup Glaze (page 39), or Chickpea Sambusaks (page 74). If you're Jewish, and like I do, identify as a member of the tribe but are lacking knowledge as to why the holidays are celebrated, read on for information from Rabbi Zoe about the holidays' place in Jewish liturgy, and from me, advice on how to plan a celebratory table of food for those holidays. If you're not Jewish, lucky you, because you have pages and pages of information that are designed bring you joy and deliciousness.

You might notice that, in some of the recipes, I repeat a few ingredients that may be as new to you as they were to me until I discovered them through my travels, especially during the several months when I lived in Morocco where the food not only of the Sephardic Jews, but also the Mizrahi Jews, has influenced the cuisine of the country; the menu choices of the ethnic restaurants—Ethiopian, Georgian, South Indian—and from various Central and South American countries, in New York City; and the recipes of some of the popular authors who through their cookbooks have directed a spotlight on their presence in food from the Middle East, North Africa, the Balkans, and Southeast Asia. I grew extremely fond of the ingredients and their capacity to transport flavor—sometimes in the most audacious ways—to create combinations that include sweet, savory, tart, and spicy in unique dishes. They may not have found a place on your spice shelf—yet—but I hope they will just as they have for me. For example, I prefer red pepper to black pepper (you certainly can use both): Aleppo pepper flakes (which are always red) bring a certain amount of heat to a dish, but they do it in a gentle, almost sweet way. I finally started to use rose harissa, and now I can't stop applying it to almost every savory dish I make. Its combination of spices that include hot peppers, garlic, cumin, caraway,

> I feel that putting together this book has comforted me and given me peace with my Jewish ancestry in ways nothing else has been able to do.

onion, and rose petals contribute their symphony of flavors to whatever they're added. I'm in love with preserved lemons on page 41, and give you a recipe for making a big jar of them to keep in your fridge to use in ways recommended in this book, and ways that you'll find on your own once you realize what the lemons, with their saltiness and citrus tang, can add to a dish. I find *labna*, a kind of yogurt cheese, to be my new best friend, whether it's an ingredient mixed with others to make a dish or serves as a platform on which other dishes rest. I've included a recipe on page 25 for you to make your own labna.

I feel that putting together this book has comforted me and given me peace with my Jewish ancestry in ways nothing else has been able to do. For years, I felt a certain sadness hearing many anti-Semitic remarks—yes, even in my small Connecticut city, a suburb of New York City, and in adulthood—just listen to the news—that sometimes made me feel awkward and a bit afraid to pronounce the beliefs of my ancestors in public. Not any more. Gosh, writing this book has underscored the fight we as Jews have fought to preserve not only religious ritual—if you like—but also certain life choices. For it begins, as with all things, food. We have to eat to carry on.

Sometimes, I call this book Hudson Valley Jewish—which, in a way it is (both Rabbi Zoe and I live here). I think of myself as a Jew of the Diaspora. I've moved around until I found a comfortable and welcoming place to land, where I make not only the food of my historic ancestors with local ingredients—just as they did—but also create new dishes that pay homage to those ingredients. You know, there was a first person who made matza ball soup. Maybe I'm the first person who made Baked Radicchio with Wheat Berries, Chickpeas, Raisins, Olives, and Feta (page 124). Maybe?

Chag Sameach. Happy Holidays.

Zoe B Zak—The Rabbi

Our sages teach that within everything there lives a Divine spark. Since being asked to write this book, my prayer has been to reveal a glimpse of the hidden sparks of each holiday and their connection to one another.

If it wasn't for Chanukah, this book wouldn't exist. I was a student at New England Conservatory of Music studying third stream music, when a fellow student posed the question: because I was Jewish, could I tell him what Chanukah was about? I knew a lot about Christianity and Hinduism, even something about Buddhism, but barely anything about my own roots, much less Chanukah. Growing up, we lit candles and received gifts. The truth was, I had no idea why and never thought to ask about the meaning of this holiday. I really didn't know what it meant to be Jewish or even how I felt about it. I'm grateful I wasn't negative about Judaism. I had no cultural baggage. Rather, my bags seemed empty, so there was plenty of room to fill them up. I don't recall the person's name or face, but I remember the moment like it was yesterday. Everything stopped: time, movement, even thoughts. There was just stillness. Something opened inside me. Something peered through a tiny crack, just long enough, as Leonard Cohen so poetically crooned, to let the light in.

I have always believed there is spiritual guidance that the One provides through endless opportunities of life's encounters. I call this The Hand of God. Surely the Divine was guiding me when I moved apartments and met my neighbor Penina, now a lifelong, treasured friend. In response to my queries, she gave me my first Jewish book, taught me how to light Shabbat candles, and explained the many dimensions of the Jewish calendar. Slowly but steadily, my inner world was shifting as I was falling in love with my own tradition. When I received my first Jewish holiday book, I was inspired to find out there was no end to the ways one might celebrate them. This led to my delving deeper and deeper to a place I came from, but never knew. Only my friend and the Holy One could see that my heart was beating faster, like a lover who met their beloved.

My Jewish journey was fueled by my conversations with Penina. I felt a growing desire for more and was drawn to attend a Shabbat service. She suggested a little shul whose services were held in a former flea market building. I went alone, I knew no one, I knew no prayers, but when they got to reciting the Shema, I wept. From that moment on, I became a sponge. I went to every service, I read the weekly Torah portion, I started practicing the holiday rituals, and most of all, I realized I was home.

In this small shul, one couldn't be invisible. I met Rabbi Jonathan Kligler, who immediately became my mentor, and we instantly connected around music. After I had attended a few services, he invited me to play my accordion before candle lighting. I played *niggunim*—wordless melodies that I had learned from attending services. Although I had been an active performing musician and recording artist, this new experience told me that I was in the right place at the right time. As I learned more and more about our tradition and its prayers, I became a lay leader, which was both thrilling and humbling. I became the rabbinic assistant, which a decade later led me to enter rabbinical school.

I entered school hungering to deepen my knowledge and acquire a strong foundation. It was sometime during my first year that my inner spark was set aflame by a deep realization of the profundity of my Jewish upbringing. Even though my parents, of blessed memory, hadn't taught me one prayer or meaning of any holiday, they lived lives modeling every Jewish foundational ethical teaching. Doing mitzvahs was their way of life. They assisted people in countless ways wherever they saw a need. I began to understand the difference between the things I was studying in my rigorous classes, and the irreplaceable things my parents had imparted to me. The essence of Judaism was in my DNA.

I've been blessed to lead services and holiday celebrations at a wide variety of places, for people of all ages and abilities. Having served Temple Israel of Catskill since 2012, I am grateful to our community that has embraced my passion for holidays and offered their partnership and support in a myriad of creative ways. They have been generous in their understanding of my personal call to spread the joy of celebrating the Jewish holidays. I have led celebrations in diverse communities; in ashrams, elder communities, and groups of people with a variety of abilities. I have been called to prisons, hospitals, hospices, and churches. A genuine connection to the holidays can be made in any place.

I have never written a book before, so when Susan Simon and Charlotte Sheedy, who I'd never met before, invited me to lunch after a Kol Nidre service they attended at the synagogue and passionately pitched the idea for this book, I felt a strong presence of The Hand of God. This opportunity offered me the chance to share my love of Judaism and Jewish celebration with a much wider audience. I just couldn't pass this up, even though while I nodded my head yes, I wondered how I would do it.

This book flows chronologically beginning with Selichot (Apology). Although Selichot is not a holiday, it is the necessary preparation for the Jewish New Year, Rosh HaShanah, and grounds us and moves us into the sacred cycle of Jewish time. Our Jewish calendar is lunisolar, balancing the solar and lunar cycles with exquisite precision. One could say that the movement of the sun and the moon is the architecture of our calendar.

The year is composed of 12 or 13 lunar months, each tracing the moon's monthly orbit around the earth. The beginning of each month signals the arrival of the new moon, when we first glimpse her appearance. As the angle changes between the earth, moon, and sun, we witness her phases. When we study the holidays, we can see that this was chosen not by happenstance but with great wisdom.

Our experiences and relationships with holidays are as individual as each one of us. Just the mere mention of Pesach (Passover) can stir excitement and joyous anticipation in one or create fear and anxiety in another. Some of us long for our childhood and devote ourselves to re-creating those experiences, whereas others are determined to create something different for themselves, their families, and friends. Some need to heal from the past, whereas others are searching to find the spark to ignite the connection for the very first time.

Our Jewish ethical foundations are embedded in the rituals that shape our holidays. Our philosophy of caring for one another and for the earth, the idea that forgiveness for both for ourselves and others, and the concept of turning and returning again to what Torah teaches us, that we were created B'tzelem Elohim, in the image of God, these are the essential strands of our holidays.

Some of us long for our childhood and devote ourselves to re-creating those experiences, whereas others are determined to create something different for themselves, their families, and friends. Some need to heal from the past, whereas others are searching to find the spark to ignite the connection for the very first time.

Following and deepening our connection to this cycle has the power to aide in the fulfillment of our life's unique mission. As idealistic as this may sound, this is my experience. By reenacting the rituals, we connect with our ancestors and create new takes, variations, and expansions on their traditions. This is not a New Age approach, but one that has existed for nearly 4,000 years as the history of our people has unfolded and our ancestors have traveled and settled throughout the world. There are no limits as to how many ways there are to access the holidays and make our own personal relationship with them uplifting, inspiring, and deeply fulfilling.

The Talmud describes Yom Kippur as one of the most joyous days of the year. Has it ever been so for you? I say, why bother having another holiday and going through all the work and huge outpouring of energy and resources if we can't be joyous about it and have a transformative experience? Can it really be? It can, and this is the perspective that calls me. Just as it takes all the members of the family to make up a family, even though we often have our favorites—and sometimes even our less favorite, it takes all the holidays to form the complete picture and unlock the mystery. This book is an invitation to enrich our holiday experiences and thread the needle of our ancestors while weaving our own tapestry.

I want to note that this book does not include the newer holidays created after the formation of the state of Israel: Yom HaShoah (Holocaust Remembrance Day), Yom HaZikaron (Israeli Memorial Day), Yom HaAtzmaut (Independence Day), and Yom Y'rushalayim (Jerusalem Day). Please consult another source to discover the power and richness of these days.

As with everything meaningful, the holidays have layers upon layers that can be gently peeled away, and there is always something new to learn, something else to ponder. I thank the Holy One for blessing me with the ability to complete this task, for having Susan as a superb book partner, and to you dear reader, for joining us on this holy journey. Together, may we go from strength to strength.

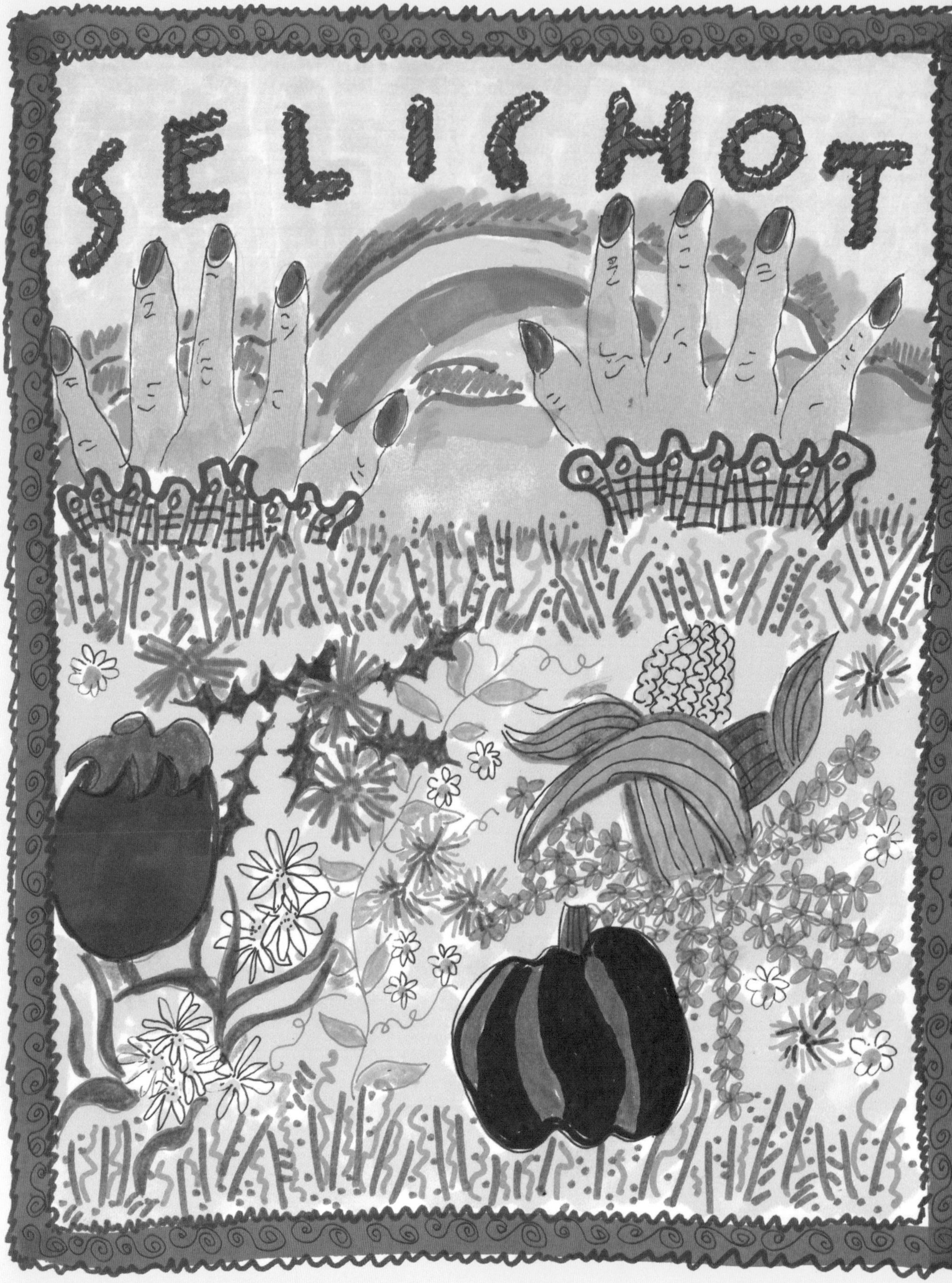
SELICHOT

CHAPTER ONE

Selichot

With the moon in her third quarter,
Selichot's midnight prayers
cry out for the opening of Heaven's Gates.

From the Rabbi

Susan: *What exactly is Selichot?*

Zoe: "Selichot" is the plural of the Hebrew word *selicha*, which translates as "apology." It's the kind of apology we make if we have spilled a drink, bumped into someone, or need to say "I'm sorry" for any reason. Selichot (Apologies) is a collection of penitential prayers and poems/hymns in which we admit our wrongdoings and plead with the Divine for forgiveness, both on a personal and communal level. "Selichot" refers both to the poems and prayers as well as to the name of the service in which we express the innermost yearnings of our hearts. In the Ashkenazic tradition, Selichot prayers begin with a contemplative and stirring midnight service, several days before Rosh HaShanah, on a Saturday night. It is said that heaven's gates are open the widest at that time.

In the Sephardic tradition, Selichot prayers begin earlier with the arrival of the Hebrew month of Elul and continue daily until Yom Kippur. This 40-day period reflects Moses's second 40-day journey atop Mount Sinai, when he pleaded with God to forgive the Israelites for worshipping the golden calf they had built while Moses was with God receiving the Ten Commandments. Torah describes that Moses's anger toward his people burned hot and how he wasn't the only one. God burned with fury, too. I love that Moses then pleads with God to turn away from God's own fierce anger and repent the evil things that the Divine was planning against the people.[1] I find this astounding, thought-provoking, and inspiring all at once. Moses used his masterful negotiating skills to convince

---

1 Exodus 32:12

the Divine that forgiveness should be given to the Israelites. He was victorious and our ancestors were forgiven.

By offering Selichot prayers, we are repeating this pattern of asking for forgiveness while tapping in to the collective memory of our people being forgiven. We take an accounting of our soul (*cheshbon hanefesh*). We look as deeply as possibly within to discover how we have missed the mark this past year, and also, to take note of the ways in which we have grown. We are told that just as the Holy One forgave our ancestors, we, too, can be forgiven and forgiving. This is how we prepare for our new year that lies closely ahead.

Are there any Selichot rituals?

There are beautiful Elul rituals and offering Selichot prayers is the way we enter the High Holidays. The prayer printed on the cover of my Selichot Sidur (Prayerbook)[2] sets the tone for all that is written between the covers:

"Creator of the Universe, I herewith forgive anyone who may have irritated, angered, or injured me, whether acting against my person, my possessions, or my reputation."

It goes on to ask that no one be punished on our behalf. We ask the Divine to keep us from repeating our mistakes and angering God. We pray that our sins be wiped away in mercy. The last line is a perfect plea:

"May the words of my mouth, and the meditations of my heart, be acceptable to You Adonai, my rock and my redeemer."[3]

Our tradition offers us many practices to guide us in our deep inner dive. During Elul, we blow the shofar every day except on Shabbat and the day before Rosh HaShanah. Although many of us are accustomed to hearing the ram's horn only on Rosh HaShanah and at the end of Yom Kippur, the monthlong custom offers a daily reminder to awaken from our inner slumber and turn our attention toward the Days of Awe.

During the month of Elul, it is a time-honored custom to visit the graves of our loved ones. There is also a tradition that if we owe an apology to someone who has died, we go to their grave and plead for forgiveness. If we are not able to do this, we send someone in our stead.

It is considered especially appropriate to give *tzedakah* (charity) during this month, as each of our actions have long-reaching influences. The Talmud explains that we should act as though we have a balance scale before us. Every mitzvah we do tips the scale to merit, affecting not only us but the entire uni-

---

2   Selichot published by the Rabbinical Assembly, 1972
3   Psalm 19:14

verse. And the opposite is true, that every transgression tips the scale against humanity.[4] What a perfect time to focus our attention on this teaching, to ready us for the new year.

Just to keep us from being too harsh with ourselves, our sages, always looking for clues to the inner meanings of everything, found this gem. In Hebrew, "Elul" is written as the letters aleph, lamed, vav, lamed. In Song of Songs, the romantic biblical love poem, there is an exquisite phrase, *Ani l'dodi v'dodi li*, which translates as "I am my beloved's and my beloved is mine."[5] The first letter of each word forms the acronym ELUL. Song of Songs is described as a love poem between the Divine and the Jewish people. I choose to read it as a love story between the Divine and all of creation. However we look at this verse, the loving eternal bond between us and our Creator is forefront and celebrated. For me, it is the perfect reminder to be as loving as possible toward myself and others as I embark upon this holy journey of *teshuvah* (to return)–to our essential being.

Because the whole month before Rosh HaShanah is used to honor Selichot rituals, would you suggest one way people prepare for the new year celebration?

Well, think of it like this: How do we prepare for any special occasion? Think of a wedding, birthday, bar mitzvah, baby naming, retirement party; think of any significant occasion that you might want to mark. We don't just show up and hope the gathering will be memorable and successful. We plan. We think of what would be meaningful, what we could do to highlight the significance of the happening. We know that some of us go to the greatest of lengths exploring every detail and that sometimes we can get lost in them. And we know that there is also a beauty and richness to be enjoyed by attending lovingly to those details.

Selichot offers us a time to really pause and reflect inwardly. If the approaching new year is really a time for potential transformation, then it will take some careful reviewing and renewing to be able to forgive ourselves and others and let go of our missteps from the previous year. It can require real focus to figure out not only who we need to ask for forgiveness, but also, what we want to say. It will take discipline to redirect and realign ourselves so that we don't retake those old missteps. If we don't do something different from what we did last year, it is unlikely that we can accomplish something different going forward.

---

4   Talmud Kiddushin 40b
5   Shir HaShirim 6:3

Our Selichot prayers help turn us toward our true God-like nature. It is here in this space that we have a chance to enact real change. Psalm 27 is among the prayers said during Selichot, and I use this verse as a mantra throughout the day during this period:

One thing have I desired of Adonai,
that I will seek after;
that I may dwell in the house of Adonai
all the days of my life,
to behold the beauty of Adonai,
and to frequent Adonai's temple.

These words embody the longing to return to our home in Adonai, that place where the Divine breathes life into us. The place where our true God-like nature is manifesting itself inwardly and outwardly. The place where we are not fighting with ourselves and one another. The repetition of these words helps me recalibrate and ready myself for what lies ahead, Rosh HaShanah. This is a time-honored method of planting spiritual seeds. I pray your garden will reap the finest of harvests.

Ketivah vachatimah tovah
May you be inscribed and sealed (in the Book of Life) for a good year!

From the Cook

Selichot is a day that recognizes, with a collection of prayers, the season that straddles the end of what we consider the summer months and the beginning of autumn, as a time when you contemplate the past year and how you'd like to improve, or continue with existent projects and thoughts, then sit with your planner and map out the year's upcoming festivities and then begin to think about how to celebrate them. Selichot has no particular celebratory food specialties. I look to suggestions from Mother Nature's late-summer bounty, then, just as Jews around the world do—prepare something special.

Pasta alla Norma
as a Room-Temperature Salad

SERVES 4

1 pound short pasta of your choice (penne, fusilli, etc.)

1 eggplant (about 1½ pounds), cut into 1½-inch chunks

½ cup olive oil, or more as needed

Salt

1 heaping tablespoon finely chopped garlic

2 teaspoons chopped fresh chiles, or 1 teaspoon dried, or more to taste (I like spicy)

1 teaspoon good-quality dried oregano

1½ to 2 pounds chopped fresh tomatoes (I use heirlooms and cherry tomatoes)

½ cup packed chopped fresh flat-leaf parsley or basil

½ cup grated ricotta salata or Pecorino Romano, plus more to taste as desired

Pasta alla Norma is a Sicilian dish that was first made to honor the composer Vincenzo Bellini the composer of the opera *Norma* and a native of Sicily's east coast. It's also a dish that celebrates the ingredients of the late-summer harvest, eggplant and tomatoes. For me, the most interesting part of this entrée is that Italian food historians, most notably Pellegrino Artusi, the late-19th-century author of the classic cookbook *Science in the Kitchen and the Art of Eating Well*, despised eggplant as the food of low-class people, "Jewish food." *Grazie mille*, Italians for ignoring the words of one of your most noted food writers and carrying on with eggplant to gift worldwide menus with eggplant Parmigiano and pasta alla Norma. I like to eat this version at room temperature on a still-warm early fall day.

1. Heat the oven to 400°F.

2. Cook the pasta in abundant boiling, salted water according to the package directions. Drain in a colander and set aside.

3. Arrange the eggplant chunks in a single layer on a parchment paper–lined rimmed baking sheet. Moisten the eggplant with a tablespoon or two of the olive oil and sprinkle with salt. Roast in the oven until nicely browned, turning occasionally, about 25 minutes. Remove from the oven and let cool.

4. Transfer the cooled pasta to a large bowl. Heat the remaining olive oil in a large skillet over medium-high heat. Add the garlic, chiles, and oregano and cook until the garlic turns pale gold. Pour the oil mixture over the pasta.

5. Add the roasted eggplant, tomatoes, and herbs to the bowl. Toss together with the other ingredients. Taste for seasoning and add more olive oil and seasonings as you like.

6. Just before serving, sprinkle with the cheese, leaving some aside for a simple garnish. Serve at room temperature.

Peperoni Mandorlati

SWEET AND SOUR PEPPERS WITH ALMONDS

SERVES 6 TO 8

2 tablespoons olive oil

1 large yellow onion, chopped coarsely

5 bell peppers, in assorted colors, sliced lengthwise into ½-inch strips—be sure to remove seeds and white membrane

1 pound plum tomatoes, peeled and chopped coarsely

¼ cup dried currants

1 tablespoon honey

1 teaspoon salt

¼ teaspoon Aleppo pepper flakes

1 tablespoon red wine vinegar

2 tablespoons freshly squeezed lemon juice

⅓ cup blanched almonds

This bell pepper recipe comes from Sicily via the Saracen invaders who brought their sweet and sour food preparations with them to the Island. I can only guess that the technique and the inclusion of almonds were influenced by the local Jewish population who were already living in Sicily when the Arabs arrived. The Jews enjoyed a tolerant relationship with their Muslim neighbors as the latter claimed Sicily as one of their emirates.

1. Heat the olive oil over medium heat in a large, heavy-bottomed, nonreactive skillet over medium heat and sauté the onion until translucent, about 3 minutes. Add the bell peppers and stir to combine. Add the tomatoes and lower the heat to medium-low, then add the currants and stir to combine. Simmer for 8 minutes.

2. While the sauce is simmering, stir together the honey, salt, Aleppo pepper flakes, vinegar, and lemon juice in a small bowl until the honey dissolves.

3. Toast the almonds in a small skillet over medium heat, until golden. Remove from the heat, let cool, and chop coarsely.

4. Remove the peppers from the heat and immediately add the vinegar mixture and toasted almonds. Stir to combine. Serve hot or at room temperature. I like to serve this as a topping for labna (see next recipe).

Zucchini and Corn Fritters
with Spicy-Garlic Labna

Think of these fritters as "beyond latkes." Fritters turn up in Jewish food as seasons and ingredient availability change. These tasty zucchini-corn fritters seem to be a good choice while corn and zucchini still fill farm stand bins. The addition of feta encourages all the other ingredients to do their best to keep up. It's worth searching for good-quality feta. Shrink-wrapped feta has zero flavor and texture. Look for feta packaged in brine, for maximum flavor.

MAKES TWELVE 2- TO 3-INCH FRITTERS, OR THIRTY TO THIRTY-TWO 1½-INCH FRITTERS

DIP

¾ cup labna (recipe follows)

1 tablespoon fruity extra-virgin olive oil

Zest and juice of 1 lime

1 garlic clove, pressed

½ teaspoon flaky sea salt

1 tablespoon finely chopped fresh dill

FRITTERS

2½ cups grated zucchini (about 2 medium zucchini; I use the big holes of a box grater)

1¼ cups fresh corn kernels (from about 2 ears)

1 large egg

½ cup all-purpose flour, plus more if needed

¾ cup crumbled feta

½ cup chopped scallions—white and pale green parts

1 tablespoon chopped fresh flat-leaf parsley

1 tablespoon chopped fresh dill

1 tablespoon chopped fresh basil

⅓ cup olive oil

⅓ cup neutral oil, such as canola

MAKE THE DIP

1. Combine the labna, olive oil, lime zest and juice, garlic, salt, and dill in a small bowl. Stir together to thoroughly mix. Cover and refrigerate.

MAKE THE FRITTERS

1. Wrap the zucchini in multiple layers of paper towels, or a clean tea towel. Squeeze to remove as much liquid as possible. Let sit while combining other ingredients.

2. Combine the corn, egg, flour, feta, scallions, parsley, dill, and basil in a large bowl. Give the zucchini another squeeze and add to the bowl. Use your hands to mix the ingredients. If the batter seems very wet, add more flour, 1 tablespoon at a time, until it binds well.

3. Heat the oils together in a large skillet over medium heat. When the oil shimmers, drop a rounded tablespoon of batter into the skillet. You should hear an immediate sizzle; if you don't, the oil isn't hot enough, so wait a moment before adding more batter. Add the batter, a tablespoon at a time, for small fritters and a 2-tablespoon scoop for larger ones. Flatten the fritters with the back of a fork and fry until golden, moving

them around and turning them over. They should cook in about 4 minutes. Carefully remove them from the oil, letting any excess oil drip back into the skillet, and transfer to a paper towel–covered tray.

4. Serve hot or at room temperature with the labna dip.

LABNA

MAKES 2 TO 3 CUPS

One 32-ounce container whole-milk Greek-style yogurt
1 teaspoon salt
1 tablespoon olive oil

I can find labna, a yogurt cheese, which I use in a variety of recipes in this book, at several shops near where I live. I'm aware that it's not available everywhere, but I'm pretty sure that plain, whole-milk Greek-style yogurt is available in most places. Here's an easy recipe to make your own labna that will keep, refrigerated, for several weeks. A good way to serve labna, when it's not being used as an ingredient, is to spread it on plate, garnish with a drizzle of olive oil and any number of other ingredients, from a simple sprinkle of the Middle East spice mixture, za'atar to a mixed, chopped salad with tomatoes, cucumbers, and fresh herbs. Then use pita bread or crackers to scoop it up.

1. Combine the yogurt, salt, and olive oil in a bowl and mix well.

2. Line a large sieve or strainer with three layers of cheese-cloth and place it over a bowl.

3. Fill the lined sieve with the yogurt mixture and gather the edges of cheesecloth together to cover the yogurt. Place a heavy object, such as a large can of tomatoes, or two smaller ones, on top of the cheesecloth and refrigerate for 24 to 48 hours. From time to time, gently press down on the refrigerated yogurt to filter out as much of the whey as possible, to achieve a thick labna.

Chocolate Angel Food Cake
with Poached Italian Plums and Plant-Based Milk Pouring Custard

**SERVES 8; MAKES ABOUT
2 CUPS CUSTARD**

CAKE

¾ cup sifted cake flour

¼ cup sifted best-quality unsweetened cocoa powder

1½ cups superfine sugar

12 room-temperature large egg whites (save yolks in groups of 3 or 4 to make the pouring custard below or ice cream, found on pages 168 and 217)

⅛ teaspoon salt

1½ teaspoons cream of tartar

½ cup chopped bittersweet chocolate

PLUMS

1 cup rosé or dry white wine

1 cup dry white vermouth

2 cups water

½ cup granulated sugar

2 pounds Italian prune plums

POURING CUSTARD

4 large egg yolks, at room temperature

2 tablespoons granulated sugar

2 cups unsweetened plant-based milk (I use oat milk)

Chocolate-covered plums have intrigued and delighted me for some time. At first, I was seduced not only by their attractive packaging but also by the thought of the combination. The product is typically Polish, and is much loved everywhere by the Jewish populations of Middle and Eastern European countries.

My chocolate angel food cake and poached Italian prune plums are my homage to the confection. The pouring custard—just a dab—adds its inimitable creaminess that pulls the dessert together. This dessert can be served following a meat or poultry meal because the milk used to make the custard is plant-based.

MAKE THE CAKE

1. Heat the oven to 375°F.

2. Combine the sifted cake flour, sifted cocoa, and half of the superfine sugar in a large bowl.

3. In the bowl of a stand mixer fitted with the whisk attachment, or in a bowl and using a hand mixer, beat together the egg whites and salt until foamy. Sprinkle the cream of tartar over them and beat until the whites hold a soft peak. Gradually beat in the remaining superfine sugar, 2 tablespoons at a time.

4. Remove the bowl from the mixer. Gradually fold in the flour mixture, about ¼ cup at a time. Fold the chopped chocolate into the batter.

5. Pour the batter into an ungreased 9-inch angel food cake pan (preferably one with feet) and bake for about 30 minutes. When the cake springs back when pressed with your finger, it's done. Remove from the oven and turn upside down to cool in the pan for at least 1 hour.

6. Tap the cake pan a few times, then use a thin knife to loosen the edges of the cake to release it.

7. The cake should be served thoroughly cooled because of the added chocolate. Use a serrated knife to cut it.

MAKE THE PLUMS

1. Combine the wine, vermouth, water, and granulated sugar in a medium-large, nonreactive pot over high heat. Bring to a boil to dissolve the sugar. Lower the heat to medium.

2. Meanwhile, rinse the plums. Cut each in half at its seam and discard the pits.

3. Lower the heat to a simmer beneath the wine mixture and add the plums. Gently poach until they are fork-tender, 15 to 30 minutes (time depends on their ripeness). Use a slotted spoon to remove the plums to a bowl.

4. Increase the heat under the remaining liquid and boil down until the consistency of maple syrup, about 20 minutes. Watch carefully as the cooking time comes to an end, as the liquid can go from just the right consistency to glue. Pour the syrup over the plums. Let cool before serving.

5. The plums can be stored in a glass container, refrigerated, for a week to 10 days.

MAKE THE CUSTARD

1. Place the egg yolks and granulated sugar in a small bowl. Whisk together until the yolks are pale and the sugar is completely incorporated, almost dissolved.

2. Heat a small saucepan over medium heat. Add the milk and scald. Remove from the heat.

3. Slowly add the scalded milk to the eggs, whisking or stirring constantly.

CONTINUES

Lactose intolerance is particularly prevalent in Jews—a high percentage of which are of Ashkenazi origin.

4. Place the pot back on the burner over medium heat. Use a wooden spoon to stir the sauce in all directions along the bottom of the pan. When it coats the back of the spoon and doesn't run off immediately, it's ready. If you notice that the sauce has slightly curdled, run it through a fine-mesh strainer.

5. Serve at room temperature or chilled, drizzled over the cake and plums. The sauce can be stored, refrigerated, for up to 4 days.

TO SERVE

1. Serve a slice of cake covered with the plums—and a splash of pouring custard, as desired.

2. The cake will keep its loft if served on the day it's baked. As it ages—if given the chance—it will condense into a thoroughly delicious, almost fudgy cake. Store in the refrigerator.

CHAPTER TWO

Rosh HaShanah

With the hope of truly beginning anew,
the moon's crescent face
sets us on our way.

From the Rabbi

Susan: *What is the meaning of Rosh HaShanah?*

Zoe: Rosh HaShanah, the Jewish New Year is a two-day Holy Time-Out-of-Time, gifted to us by the Divine. We celebrate the birthday of the world, eat festive meals, and wish one another other New Year's blessings. We do everything we can to fulfill the mitzvah to hear the shofar (ram's horn), so that we might be awakened by its cry.

Imagine being able to leave last year's regrets with last year. To do that, we continue the process of self-reflection begun last month, making all apologies that are needed. We go outside to the water for Tashlich, casting away our misdeeds and regrets. We give thanks to the Divine for being a merciful Creator and pray to be forgiven for our wrongdoings. We call out, "Remember us for Life and write us into the Book of Life." We pray to have the opportunity to live another year and serve our Creator with all our hearts and all our might.

People seem to be confused about the beginning of the Jewish new year. Please explain the difference between the Hebrew and Gregorian calendars.

The easy answer is, the New Year does not fall during the month of January because we use a Hebrew calendar. The Torah tells us that it was during the Hebrew month of Nissan, which falls in the springtime, when our ancestors were still in the land of Egypt, that they received their first commandment: "And God said to Moses . . . This month is for you, the head of the months, it is first for you among the months of the year."[6]

Torah refers to months of the year by number and Nissan is number one (*rishon*, the first). When our calendar was set in the fourth century by rabbis, they established the Hebrew month of Tishrei as the first month of the year. What is important here is that the first of Tishrei was established as Rosh HaShanah (Head of the Year), even though it is technically the seventh month of the year.

In our tradition, seven is a very special number, representing completion. Shabbat, our week's crowning glory, is the seventh day of the week. Rosh HaShanah, Yom Kippur, and the festival of Sukkot all take place in the seventh month of Tishrei. In Israel, the Sabbatical Year—when the land is given a rest—occurs every 7 years, and after 49 years (7 × 7), the Jubilee Year—where the land reverts to its original owner—is celebrated in the 50th year. When Rosh HaShanah begins, we are not only tapping in to a long and rich history of this holiday, but in to a larger rhythm of the history of our people's cycles of ritual.

Is the shofar only used to welcome Rosh HaShanah?

Hearing the shofar is the central mitzvah of Rosh HaShanah. As a matter of fact, the only instruction Torah gives us about this day is for it to be a Shabbat Shabbaton—a glorious Shabbat where we blow the shofar and do no work.[7] There are differing opinions on how many times the shofar is to be blown during each of the two days of services, but 100 is the most agreed-upon number.

The shofar is usually made from a hollowed-out ram's horn; however, a variety of other kosher animals' horns can be used. My favorite one is an exceptionally long and gracefully twisted horn of a kudu, an African antelope. A beloved congregant and his eight-year-old son gifted this to me several years ago during our Children's Service on Rosh HaShanah. It had belonged to the little boy's great-grandfather and I treasure it.

For years now, I've been calling the shofar "the Jewish alarm clock." After all, who could even think of sleeping through such a wailing, primordial cry? On Rosh HaShanah, its function is to awaken us. We offer four shofar sounds of varying lengths on Rosh HaShanah. There are beautiful teachings about the meanings of the sounds and how they stir, awaken, and encourage us. I think of parents and teachers who speak to each child differently because they don't all absorb information in the same way. Different words and explanations are

---

6 Exodus 12:1–2
7 Leviticus 23:24

needed to reach different people. In the case of the shofar, one sound may stir one person but not another. I believe they exist to offer us as many access points as possible, to make sure that each of us is reached by the call of the shofar.

Throughout our people's history, the shofar has played a significant role. In ancient days, the shofar was blown to announce the king's coronation. Before that, it was blown at the giving of the Torah on Mount Sinai. It was sounded in battles as a warning, and the sages teach that when we blow the shofar we are proclaiming God as our Sovereign. It is written that the shofar will be sounded when Mashiach (the Messiah) comes.[8] The shofar is sounded on both days of Rosh HaShanah, unless one of them is Shabbat, and then it is not blown. It is also sounded triumphantly at the conclusion of Yom Kippur.

Remember Joshua, the one who fought the battle of Jericho? God spoke to him, saying he should encompass the city for six days. Each day, he, and his troops, blew their shofars while circling. The rest of the people were directed to await their future in utter silence, and for seven days they did just that. On the seventh day, the troops were to circle seven times with the seven priests again blowing their shofars. The people were to listen for the one long blast, and when they heard it, they were instructed to shout with all their might. We know from the song "The Battle of Jericho" that when these directives were followed, "the walls came tumblin' down."[9]

Why are there multiple names for the New Year?

Torah names this day Yom Teru'ah (Day of Teru'ah[10] or Day of Shofar Blowing). In our Machzor, our High Holiday prayer book, we have prayers referring to this day as Yom HaZikaron (Day of Remembrance) and Yom HaDin (Day of Judgment). The one we most often use is Rosh HaShanah, so named in the Mishnah.[11] We have even more names when you consider the entire 10-day period from Rosh HaShanah through Yom Kippur, the 1st through 10th of the Hebrew month of Tishrei. We call this period Yamim Nora'im (Days of Awe); we might say the Awesome Days, or as many do, the High Holidays or the High Holy Days.

These names represent different aspects of the holiday. They also reflect the evolution of both its meaning and the way it has been celebrated over time. Names are important and each offers us a unique access code to the holiday. Perhaps thinking of this day as the Day of Judgment feels too severe for someone, but the Day of Shofar Blowing really speaks to them. Many of our holidays have

8 Isaiah 27:13
9 Joshua 6:20
10 Numbers 29:1
11 Mishnah, Rosh Hashanah 1:1

multiple names, each inviting us to enter through a different door, each of them beautiful, each of them valid, and each of them a part of a larger full experience.

What exactly is Tashlich?

"Tashlich" is a Hebrew word meaning "cast," as in to cast away what we do not want. The prophet Micah said, "You will cast all their sins into the depths of the sea."[12] Ezekiel said, "Cast away yourselves all your transgressions, and create within yourself a new heart and new spirit."[13] These teachings inspired a new ritual, one that invites various creative approaches.

Tashlich takes place on Rosh HaShanah afternoon, or on the second day if the first day is Shabbat. My community gathers at Catskill Point, where the Catskill Creek flows into the Hudson River. Some people have the custom to empty their pockets, as though releasing anything left over from the previous year. The tradition was to cast bread into the water until the environmentalist taught us that this was not healthy for the fish. As an alternative, many people now cast birdseed into the water. We offer up all that we wish to forgive ourselves, all that we pray to be forgiven for; we offer it all to HaShem (The Name), The One who is infinite enough to receive all our regrets.

I've heard people give different greetings on Rosh HaShanah. What should we say?

Sometimes, we think we have finally cracked the code and know how to offer the right greeting. Then someone comes along and calls out words we aren't familiar with, and all we can do is respond with a blank stare. When I was growing up, my parents always said, "Good Yontiff," the English-Yiddish expression that means "(May you have) a good holiday." I had no idea there was another way, much less a variety of ways to bless one another during the Yamim Nora'im (Days of Awe). The important thing is to be able to extend a heartfelt greeting without worrying you might not get it right. My suggestion is to just say what you want to say from your heart. However, if you want the inside scoop, here it is.

To begin with, we can always say, "Shanah Tovah" ("Happy New Year") or enhance it with "Shanah Tovah U'Metetuka" ("[May you have] a Sweet and Happy New Year"). Prior to Rosh HaShanah, we say, "Ketivah v'Chatima Tovah" ("[May you have] a Good Inscription and Sealing [in the Book of Life]"). Hebrew, being a gender-specific language, has thus far offered two greetings on Erev Rosh

---

12 Micah 7:19
13 Ezekiel 18:31

HaShanah, the eve of our holiday: "L'Shanah Tovah Tikatev v'Tichatem" (m) or "L'Shanah Tovah Tikatevee v'Tichatemee" (f) ("[May you] Be Written and Sealed [in the Book of Life] for a Good Year"). If you are looking for a gender-neutral blessing, we can always say "Shanah Tovah U'Metukah." From Rosh HaShanah day until Yom Kippur, we say, "Gemar Chatimah Tovah" ("[May you have] a Good and Final Sealing [in the Book of Life]!").

Many people offer Yiddish blessings. "Gut Yontiff" ("A Good Holiday") can be extended to "A Gut Gebentsht Yohr" ("[May you have] a Good and Blessed Year"). May all these blessings be yours!

It is fascinating that immediately following Rosh HaShanah, Tzom Gedaliah (Fast of Gedaliah) is observed. This is a dawn-to-dusk fast on the third of Tishrei unless that day is Shabbat, in which case it is moved to Sunday. Special Selichot prayers, ones pleading to God for forgiveness for our misguided ways, are offered.

After the destruction of the First Temple in Jerusalem by the Babylonians, most of the Jews had been exiled. Governor Gedaliah was appointed to oversee the remnants of our people still in the Holy Land, in the province of Judea. He helped to both unify the people and heal the land, which, like the people, had suffered greatly from all the fighting. He had been warned that a jealous rival was out to kill him, but he did not heed the warning and was subsequently brutally murdered. More bloodshed followed suit and the remaining Jews all went into exile.

The destruction of the temple, and the exile of the people, meant the exile of the Holy One. You can read more about this in Chapter 13, which discusses Tisha B'Av. The devastation and sense of inner and outer loss was monumental.

A most remarkable aspect of our tradition is that we are a hopeful people to the core of our souls. There are countless examples of this in our history, liturgy, and rituals. The prophet Zechariah summed this up perfectly when he said that all fasts "will become times of joy and gladness . . . therefore love, truth, and peace."[14] May it be so, speedily and in our day.

14   Zechariah 8:19

From the Cook

Rosh HaShanah is one of the Jewish holidays that is more known to me. I figure that there's no better time to celebrate the New Year than the end of a lazy summer and the beginning of fall, when everything seems to get into gear again. Most notably included on Jewish holiday tables are recently harvested apples and honey, whether it's sliced apples dipped into honey to ensure a sweet new year, or the ingredients combined with others to produce an apple cake. My Israeli friends think of pomegranates when Rosh HaShanah arrives—fortunate them—they have an almost year-round harvest of the fruit filled with jewel-like arils that symbolizes the richness of the Promised Land. The expansive recognition of Rosh HaShanah as an important holiday on the Jewish calendar is probably a result of media coverage through newspapers that spotlight holiday recipes in their food sections, and on the televised news programs that briefly describe the holiday's significance.

Chestnut and Chickpea Soup

SERVES 4 TO 6

8 ounces dried Italian chestnuts (imported Italian chestnuts may come in a 250-gram package, closer to 9 ounces; that is OK)

¼ cup extra-virgin olive oil, plus more to finish

2 garlic cloves, peeled

1 rosemary sprig, plus more for garnish (optional)

4 juniper berries

Two 15.5-ounce cans chickpeas, undrained

2 cups stock (I use vegetable)

Grated Grana Padano or Parmigiano for serving

When the Italian mother of a Hudson Valley friend came from her home in Milano for a three-months-long visit with her son, she kindly brought me a couple of bags of dried Italian chestnuts, and a recipe that includes not only chestnuts but also chickpeas to make this hearty soup. Olga spent a day in my kitchen showing me how to put together this recipe, and a few others, too. I'm forever grateful.

Olga makes a clear distinction between a *zuppa*, a hearty, dense soup, and a *minestra*, also a soup but one that has a more liquid base. This one's a zuppa.

1. Soak the chestnuts in cold water to cover for at least 12 hours or overnight.

2. Heat the olive oil in a large pot over medium-high heat. When the oil is hot, add the whole garlic cloves, rosemary, and juniper berries and sauté until the garlic is pale gold, about 2 minutes.

Chestnuts appear on Rosh HaShanah menus in dishes from Hungary to Italy. You are likely to find chestnuts in a Hungarian-style brisket where they crumble into the sauce, giving it heft and a touch of sweetness. In Italy, origin of the world's best chestnuts, in my opinion, find chestnuts in pastries for Rosh HaShanah, and in *charoset* on Passover. Chestnut flour is used to make *castagnaccio*—a cake that can be sweet with added pine nuts and raisins, or savory with fresh rosemary—and for Marrons Glacés (candied chestnuts), one of my top 10 favorite foods.

CONTINUES

37

Chickpeas are among the most ancient of cultivated legumes. The chickpea shows itself as the star of falafel (a fried chickpea and fresh herb fritter) and hummus, both of which originated in Middle Eastern countries and became popular in Israel.

3. Remove the garlic. Add the chickpeas and their liquid. Add the stock and drained chestnuts. Lower the heat to medium-low and simmer until the chestnuts are almost falling-apart tender, 45 minutes to 1 hour. You may need to add more stock if the zuppa gets too thick.

4. Serve hot with a shower of grated cheese and a drizzle of extra-virgin olive oil. Garnish with additional rosemary, if desired.

Roasted Chicken *with Apricot Butter–Maple Syrup Glaze*

SERVES 3 TO 4

2 medium yellow onions, sliced thinly (2 heaping cups)

Heaping ½ cup thinly sliced shallots

6 to 8 fresh sage leaves

¼ cup olive oil

2 teaspoons salt

One 3½-pound chicken

⅓ cup pure maple syrup

½ cup Apricot Butter (page 198)

1 teaspoon rose harissa

Here's a Hudson Valley twist on a favorite food often served on Jewish tables: roast chicken. The perfect recipe for Apricot Butter (page 198) lends its smooth texture and slightly tart flavor to local maple syrup to make just the right glaze for a roast chicken. And, of course, a bit of rose harissa takes away any possibility of the bird's being too cloyingly sweet. I like to roast chicken in a cast-iron skillet. It stays cozy with all the other ingredients, leading to optimal flavor.

1. Heat the oven to 400°F.

2. Combine the onions, shallots, sage, olive oil, and 1 teaspoon of the salt in a bowl and toss together.

3. Truss the chicken by tying its thighs together at the bone joint, tucking the tip of each wing under the meaty part, and securing both wings to the body of the chicken. Stuff about one-third of the onion mixture into the cavity of the chicken. Put the remainder into a large cast-iron skillet. Use your hands to rub some of the onion oil over the chicken.

4. Roast the chicken in the oven for 20 minutes. Meanwhile, combine the maple syrup, apricot butter, rose harissa, and remaining teaspoon of salt in a small bowl and mix together.

5. Lower the oven temperature to 325°F and roast the chicken for an additional 15 minutes.

6. Spoon the glaze all over the surface of the chicken. Roast for 45 minutes more, or until an instant-read thermometer inserted into the thickest part of the chicken (the breast) registers 165°F.

7. Remove from the oven. Let rest for 10 minutes. Serve.

Berenjena

FRIED EGGPLANT DRIZZLED WITH HONEY AND PRESERVED LEMONS

SERVES 4 TO 6

2 purple eggplants
(1½ pounds total), or
4 Japanese eggplants,
edges trimmed, cut
crosswise on the bias to
about ¼ inch thick, or into
¼-inch rounds or ¾-inch
matchsticks

2½ cups whole milk
(optional)

2 tablespoons kosher salt
(1 tablespoon optional)

Neutral oil, such as canola oil,
for frying

1 cup all-purpose flour

3 tablespoons runny honey

2 tablespoons finely diced
Preserved Lemons (recipe
follows) or flaky sea salt

This *berenjena* (eggplant) recipe is a specialty of southern Spain, in the Andalusia region, where a majority of the Jews lived. Most recipes for this dish ask for a sprinkling of sea salt on the honey to finish. I turn to a preserved lemon finish, which not only brings a satisfying saltiness to the dish, but also the bright tang of citrus.

1. If your eggplant doesn't come fresh from your garden, or at least off a farmers' market table, where bitterness is a nonexistent problem, place the eggplant pieces in a bowl and cover with the milk and 1 tablespoon of the salt to help remove the bitterness. Cover the bowl and refrigerate for at least 2 hours.

2. Heat about an inch of oil in a large, heavy-bottomed skillet over medium-high heat.

3. Spread the flour on a large plate or tray and mix with the remaining tablespoon of salt. Dredge the eggplant pieces in the flour, shaking away the excess. Working in batches, fry the eggplant, turning a few times until golden on all sides, 3 to 4 minutes. Transfer to a paper towel–lined tray.

4. Place the fried eggplant on a serving platter, drizzle with the honey, and garnish with diced preserved lemons or flaky sea salt. Serve immediately.

Just like the Italian Jews who loved eggplant, and were despised for it, the Spanish Jews became so associated with the use of eggplant in their *cocina* that it was used against them during the Inquisition trials. The Spanish court would track Jews by following the food they bought and consumed. Following their expulsion from Spain, some Jews migrated to Italy, and their love of eggplant came with them, prompting the quote from Pellegrino Artusi mentioned on page 22.

PRESERVED LEMONS

6 lemons

3 cups kosher salt

3 tablespoons sugar

½ cup freshly squeezed
  lemon juice

Preserved lemons were most likely developed in North Africa, specifically Morocco, where lemons abound. Preserving them in salt and sugar is a way to hold on to them as an ingredient whenever needed. Because Jewish cooking is actually the food of where Jewish populations lived, combined with kosher dietary law—preserved lemons are a popular ingredient of the Jews of Israel. This recipe was put together by my dear friend Cary Guy.

1. Quarter four of the lemons, slicing toward the stem end without cutting through the bottoms. Fully quarter the two remaining lemons.

2. Stir together the salt and sugar in a large bowl. Add the four partially quartered lemons and pack the salt in and around them.

3. Transfer the salted lemons to a large mason jar, or two smaller ones. Fill in the empty spaces with the single pieces of quartered lemon and any leftover salt mixture. Pour the lemon juice over the top.

4. Leaving them out at room temperature, turn the jars every day for 2 weeks. Then, refrigerate. They will keep, refrigerated, for many months.

5. To use: Work with a quarter of a lemon at a time. Use a sharp paring knife to remove the pulp and then the pith. Dice the skin to the desired size.

Scarpazza

This recipe was created by the renowned 16th-century Italian chef Bartolomeo Scappi. While Scappi's original *cucina* relied on unexpected combinations of ingredients, usually at the service of banquets for the Catholic Church, he was particularly complementary to the Jews when he lauded "the liver of domestic geese raised by the Jews is of extreme size." A way of fattening up geese came to Italy with Egyptian Jews. *Scarpazza*, a Scappi creation, doesn't have goose liver in it, but it does have his signature whimsical mix of ingredients that may well have come to Italy with the Jews when they arrived from North Africa with their love of spinach used in New Year's food (along with leeks and chard), their spices, and their geese.

SERVES 8 TO 10

2 thickly cut slices dense Mediterranean-style bread, crusts removed, cut into 1-inch chunks

1 cup whole milk

1½ pounds fresh spinach, tough stems removed, rinsed

6 tablespoons (¾ stick) unsalted butter, plus more for baking dish

1 teaspoon salt

¼ cup raisins

¼ cup grated Grana Padano or Parmigiano

4 amaretti cookies, crushed

1 teaspoon ground cinnamon

¼ teaspoon freshly ground black pepper

4 large eggs, lightly beaten

1 tablespoon pine nuts

2 tablespoons unseasoned bread crumbs

1. Place the bread and milk in a bowl and let soak for at least 30 minutes.

2. Combine the rinsed, but not dried, spinach leaves in a large saucepan or deep skillet over medium-low heat. Use a wooden spoon to stir them around the pan. When they've wilted, remove from the heat. When they are cool enough to handle, chop coarsely.

3. Melt 4 tablespoons of the butter in a medium skillet over medium heat. Add the chopped spinach and sprinkle the flour over it, stir to combine, then sauté for 5 minutes. The flour may begin to stick after a few minutes; continue to stir. Add the bread and milk and stir for another 3 to 4 minutes, until the mixture begins to tighten up and the milk has been absorbed. Remove from the heat.

4. Add the raisins, cheese, crushed amaretti, cinnamon, and pepper. Mix to thoroughly incorporate. Add the eggs and combine.

5. Heat the oven to 350ºF. Butter a 9½-inch pie or quiche dish. Transfer the spinach mixture to the dish and evenly distribute. Press down firmly to even out the tart. Sprinkle the pine nuts over the top. Spoon bread crumbs over the top and dot with the 2 remaining tablespoons of butter. Bake for 30 minutes, or until set in the center of the tart.

6. Serve hot or at room temperature. Cut into larger pieces to serve as a brunch main dish, or into smaller pieces to be part of an appetizer plate.

Eden's Applesauce

**MAKES APPROXIMATELY
5 PINTS**

6 pounds assorted apples
[I use Gala and Mutsu]

2 or more cups liquid [water,
cider, or juice (or more as
needed); I use Samascott's
apple cider]

⅓ cup cinnamon sugar
[I use 2 teaspoons ground
cinnamon mixed with
⅓ cup sugar]

½ teaspoon butter [I use
1 teaspoon unsalted
butter]

Dash of salt

Optional: if you can find a
quince, wash it, cut it, and
add it to the pot. It will
make the sauce pink and
sweeter [Eden's addition]

NOTE: *I froze, in pint-size
containers, the applesauce
that I didn't immediately
consume.*

Another recipe for apples, one of the stars of Rosh
HaShanah menus. This one is from Eden Ross Lipson, of
blessed memory, who was my neighbor and my friend.
She was also the children's book editor at the *New York
Times* for 20 years. Her posthumously published book
Applesauce Season was her lasting gift for her adored
young readers. When I was putting together recipes for
this book, I knew that Eden's applesauce recipe had to be
included. I asked her daughter Margo whether I could use
the recipe. Knowing that I would be using storage apples
to test the recipe, she answered, "Of course, you should use
Eden's recipe! To be honest my Eden [her daughter] loves
applesauce so much I've made it wildly out of season but
I'm sure my mother wouldn't mind and bless Samascott
for their excellent cold storage and keeping apples tasty
almost year 'round."

Samascott Orchards is the source of my apples, too. Their
apple trees and farm store are here in the Hudson Valley,
and they've occupied the northwest corner of Union Square
Saturday Farmers' Market in New York City for decades.

This is the recipe copied verbatim from Eden's book. I've
included my notes (in square brackets) as well.

1. Wash and cut up the apples. [Eden's recipe includes the
   core and the seeds. I cored the apples and left the skin on.]

2. Put the apples in a heavy [nonreactive] saucepan [I used
   a 5-quart stockpot]. Add the liquid [and cinnamon sugar]
   and cover [I cooked it uncovered]. Cook at a medium
   flame until soft and foamy—about 20 minutes.

3. Remove from flame, uncover [add the butter and salt],
   and let cool briefly, but while still warm transfer the
   apple mixture [in batches] to a food mill placed over a
   large bowl. Grind down thoroughly.

4. The sauce will be loose, even runny. It will thicken as it
   cools. Season to taste. Serve warm or cold.

Apple Iced Tea

This tea combines apples and honey to make an appropriate and refreshing holiday beverage.

SERVES 4

4 cups water

2 tea bags of your choice
(I like English universal tea
brands, such as PG Tips or
Typhoo; you may prefer
the smoky Earl Grey)

1 cinnamon stick

4 cups sweet apple cider

1 to 2 tablespoons runny
honey

1 lemon, sliced thinly, seeds
removed

2 sweet, crisp apples (I like
Gala), cored, quartered,
and sliced thinly

1 tablespoon freshly
squeezed lemon juice

Optional garnish: fresh mint
sprigs

1. Bring 4 cups of water to boil in a large saucepan and add the tea bags. Remove from the heat and let the tea steep for 20 minutes. Remove the tea bags.

2. Add the cinnamon stick, apple cider, honey, lemon slices, and stir well to dissolve the honey. Leave at room temperature to infuse for at least 8 hours, or overnight.

3. Cover the sliced apples with the lemon juice. Set aside.

4. To Serve: Fill tall glasses with ice and pour in the tea. Garnish with the apple slices and fresh mint sprigs, if using.

For Ashkenazi Jews, a plate of sliced apples and a bowl of honey on the Rosh HaShanah table are an absolute. Diners dip a crispy slice of apple into the honey to ensure a sweet and prosperous/fruitful New Year.

CHAPTER THREE

Yom Kippur

Like a baby bump and still in her first quarter,
longing to grow and fulfill her greatest potential,
we turn inward deepening our gaze.

From the Rabbi

Susan: *Why is Yom Kippur considered the holiest holiday?*

Zoe: Yom Kippur receives its status of being the holiest day of the year from Torah. We read that the 10th of the Hebrew month of Tishrei is a Shabbat Shabbaton (Shabbat of Shabbats).[15] "And this shall be an everlasting statute to you, to make *teshuvah* [atonement] return, for the people of Israel for all their sins [misdeeds], once a year.[16] While growing up, I thought it was odd that Judaism set aside one day to ask for forgiveness. Even as a kid, I knew we humans needed more than that. Attending my first *mincha* (afternoon prayer service), as an adult, I found myself praying the Amidah, "Bring us back to You in true teshuvah. Blessed are you Adonai, who welcomes teshuvah!"[17] Continuing, I found familiar words from our High Holiday liturgy, "Forgive us our parent, for we have sinned against you." The blessing ends, "Blessed are you Adonai, who is quick to forgive."[18] Our tradition is so brilliant, building into our daily prayers, a way of asking for forgiveness.

This experience encapsulates my ongoing learning about the intricacies and thoughtfulness that weave throughout Jewish tradition. Discovering that we pray for forgiveness each and every day was, for me, akin to placing a missing cosmic puzzle piece in its perfect spot. I'm so grateful we have a tradition that

---

15 Leviticus 23:32
16 Leviticus 23:32
17 Amidah, Fifth Blessing
18 Amidah, Sixth Blessing

recognizes our humanness and how easily we misstep. I'm comforted by Yom Kippur, when all our prayers for teshuvah culminate. On that day, we are met face to face with the essence of forgiveness and repair, and we can experience the transformative power of the Divine.

Is there a forgiveness story that anchors this day?

We read in the Torah that, after Moses had been called by the Divine to ascend Mount Sinai, our ancestors, waiting at the base of the mountain, lost faith and turned their attention away from God. Gold jewelry was gathered by members of the tribe and the golden calf was formed from the burning fires, becoming the embodiment of their devastating loss. The bottom line is that our predecessors were forgiven, not only by Moses who saw their humanity, but by God, though not without a fight. Moses pleaded for their lives with lawyerlike precision and won over God, who had threatened to destroy our people for their transgressions. On this day, our ancestors were gifted the second set of tablets, a new beginning, a renewed covenant. Just before that, the Holy One descended in a cloud and proclaimed, "Adonai, Adonai is compassionate and gracious, slow to anger, abounding in kindness and faithfulness, extending kindness to the thousandth generation, forgiving iniquity, transgression and sin."[19] These are the Middot HaRachamim (Thirteen Attributes of Mercy), central to both Rosh HaShanah and Yom Kippur services. Some say, that by offering these words, that like Moses, we are hoping to appease and influence the Holy One so we may be forgiven. The Kabbalists teach that we say these words to inspire us to emulate God's qualities, much like the inner work we do during Sefirat HaOmer (see Chapter 11). Chanting The Thirteen Attributes has always been a high point of High Holy Day services for me. When singing this and Avinu Malkeinu, it has always felt that the community is singing with one voice. May it be so this year and always.

What is the Book of Life that we are asking to be inscribed in, and does it have relevance for the 21st-century person?

In the aforementioned Torah story, Moses pleaded to God with all his heart to forgive the Israelites. He told God, if you can't forgive the people, "blot me from The Book which you have written."[20]

I think of The Book as a metaphorical, metaphysical book, a spiritual place. Longing to be written in this Book of Life, is a longing to be given the gift of

---

19   Exodus 34:6
20   Exodus 32:32

another year of life to get even closer to be the best version of ourselves that we can be.

There are many inspiring stories about the teachings of Reb Zusha, an 18th-century Chassidic sage. One that really speaks to your question follows.

Reb Zusha was known to think a great deal about the end of life, and when he finally reached that moment, he was trembling with fear. His students who were beside him asked what he was so afraid of. "I am not afraid of being asked why I was not Moses, after all, God already has a Moses. I am afraid, however, of being asked, 'Zusha, why weren't you Zusha?'"

We pray to be worthy of another year, to make our amends, to forgive those who have wronged us, to be forgiven by the people we have wronged and by the Creator. We pray to reset our course and to rededicate our lives so that we may fulfill our greatest potential of becoming fully ourselves.

Do I really have to fast to have the full-on Yom Kippur experience?

I'm appreciative of this question as it is something I give a lot of thought to each year. Usually, there is a peanut butter and jelly sandwich in my *tallit* (prayer shawl) bag, that at some point I sneak away to eat. I have low blood sugar, so it just isn't feasible for me to fast. Many people are unable to fast for various health reasons and it is important that they do not feel guilty in any way about this.

Rabbi Simcha Y. Weintraub has written a wonderful "Meditation Before Yom Kippur for One Who Cannot Fast":

> *May my eating be as a fast;*
> *May it be dedicated to You, to T'shuvah–*
> *To the renewal and restoration of my Relationship*
> *To You, to Others and to Myself.*[21]

Rabbi Hannoch Hecht writes in his inspired book, *The Kabbalah of Food*, "Eating can accomplish the same desired outcome as fasting."[22] The most important thing whether we fast or eat, is that we dedicate it to the Divine.

Maimonides said, "If ninety-nine doctors say it is OK to fast, but one says that it is not, you shouldn't fast."

This day's fast is the most intense one of the year–a 25-hour fast that prohibits drinking even water, wearing leather shoes, wearing lotions or perfumes, bathing, or having intimate relations. Traditionally men wear a *kittel* (a long white

---

21 Published by Jewish Board of Family and Children's Services
22 Monkfish Publishing Company, 2020

robe) or white clothing instead of our usual festive holiday clothing. Others have also adopted this practice and it is often the *minhag* (the custom) in many communities. The kittel is a symbol of the shroud we will someday be buried in and wearing it shows our recognition of the fragility of life.

Many years ago, I visited a friend's shul on Yom Kippur. I wore the plainest of white dresses, cloth sneakers, hadn't showered, no makeup, and of course, no jewelry. Having learned this was the custom on Yom Kippur, and as an adult only having attended my own shul during the High Holy Days, I was thoroughly unprepared for what I experienced.

> Teshuvah is a spiritual process, a way of life, a way of love, a way to God. It is a way to turn from where we are and in turning, return to the Divine and our true nature of being B'tzelem Elohim, created in the image of the Divine.

Everyone was dressed in their finest clothing, shoes, jewelry, wearing makeup and even perfume. I was not only embarrassed but confused. I also could feel the temptation rising within me to judge this community as if I held the key to knowing how to observe Yom Kippur the correct way. This experience was a reminder of something I regularly taught but momentarily had lost sight of, that there are many ways to observe and honor every one of our holidays. If there are keys, the only One who holds them is the One.

What is Teshuvah?

Teshuvah is a spiritual process, a way of life, a way of love, a way to God. It is a way to turn from where we are and in turning, return to the Divine and our true nature of being B'tzelem Elohim, created in the image of the Divine. "At present, when the temple does not exist and there is no altar of atonement, there remains nothing else aside from teshuvah."[23] This statement by Maimonides, the renowned medieval scholar and physician, also known as Rambam, says it all. If we could do only one thing, teshuvah is most important. Returning to our true God-like nature is, of course, easier said than done. To accomplish this, we need to make the best choices possible in every aspect of our lives. Imagine if we conducted ourselves as though every action we took, whether in public or private, had a consequence not only for ourselves but for the entire world. This is our aspiration, and this is Rambam's guidance on how to accomplish that.

We should view ourselves and the world alike as being equally balanced between merit and sin. When we do a mitzvah, we tip our own and the world's balance to the side of merit, which brings deliverance and salvation. When we

---

23 Mishnah Torah 1:3

sin, we tip the balance in that direction, and bring guilt and destruction upon ourselves.[24]

Another way we aim to tip the scales toward merit is by giving tzedakah, which means, in addition to "charity," "righteousness." It is considered the natural order of things to share what we have with others and this is encouraged year-round. During Aseret Yemai Teshuvah (The Ten Days of Teshuvah, or The Days of Awe), it is customary to increase our giving of tzedakah, monetary gifts and other mitzvahs that can always be done in honor or memory of someone. We have the choice to choose to do teshuvah and to create for ourselves a better outcome. It is about free will—the freedom to align ourselves with HaShem, with doing mitzvahs that bring us and keep us close with HaShem. This all embodies the powerful redemption that Yom Kippur has to offer.

Why is a memorial service held on Yom Kippur?

Our sages in their wisdom, taught us to set aside time to create space for a Yizkor (Memorial Service), to remember those who have passed. This occurs four times a year: on Yom Kippur and during the three festivals of Sukkot, Pesach, and Shavuot. See page 82 to find out more about this incredibly important custom that offers tremendous comfort.

While growing up, once or twice a year on Rosh HaShanah and Yom Kippur, I attended services with my parents at Congregation Beth Emeth in Albany, New York. When it was time for Kaddish Yatom (The Mourner's Kaddish), my father went to a place deep within himself that I could viscerally feel and that profoundly comforted me. I could never forget that feeling or how it bound me to my father, the one I looked up to, admired, and committed myself to be as much like as possible.

I heard you once say something about dying on Yom Kippur. Can you tell me if I heard you correctly?

Maimonides taught, "A person should always view himself as leaning towards death, with the possibility that he might die at any time."[25] I believe this was meant to encourage us to rush to do mitzvot and to do teshuvah, because we don't know when it will be our time. None of us knows when we will die.

There is a certain kind of death that can happen by the end of Yom Kippur. After all the prayers, the fasting, the pleading, there is a release, there is a change, something moved, something within us shifted. We now come to our

---

24 Maimonides, Mishneh Torah Chapter 3:4, Hilchot Teshuvah (Laws of Repentance)
25 Maimonides, Mishnah Torah—Hilchot Teshuvah 7:2

final three prayers, and they are the very same ones that we pray immediately when someone has died.

We chant once: *Sh'ma Yisrael, Adonai Eloheynu, Adonai Echad.* (Listen Israel, Adonai is our God, Adonai is One.)

We chant three times: *Baruch shem k'vod malchuto l'olam va'ed.* (Blessed is God's glorious majesty forever and ever.)

We chant seven times: *Adonai hu haElohim.* (Adonai is God.)

To me, this is the most profound punctuation that a Yom Kippur service could possibly have. When I am chanting them before the congregation, it is a sacred time of utter awe and wonder. One powerful, long, final blast of the shofar follows, and our sages tell us, this shofar blast will be heard when the Messiah comes and brings about Messianic peace. This isn't something that will just happen to us. We must continue our work that we have been doing throughout these holidays, to help bring about this time we long for.

We then make Havdalah, the sensuous ritual that ends the holiday. We light the wicks of a braided candle; we make blessings over wine, spices, and the flames. This ritual helps to bring us back down to earth as we anticipate breaking our fast. Immediately afterward, we go outside to where our *sukkah* will be built and take one action that begins the building of the sukkah. Talk about connecting our holidays to one another—there is nothing more visceral than this. The joy of Sukkot is around the corner, and we waste no time in readying ourselves to fulfill this mitzvah.

When we wonder, did we fulfill the Mishnah's directive for this day to be joyous, consider what it feels like to be forgiven and what it feels like to forgive someone else. It is astoundingly liberating. It is as though we had knowingly or unknowingly carried around all this extra weight, like weighted suitcases and wearing backpacks loaded down with the heaviest of objects and then in a moment's notice, they were lifted. It is because being forgiven and forgiving is essential to being whole and being healed and moving forward with our lives. This is the joy of Yom Kippur.

From the Cook

Erev Yom Kippur—Eve of Yom Kippur

Besides being a time to fill your belly in preparation for a fast, the evening was the genesis—an appropriate biblical reference—of this book. A few friends and I made the trip across the river from our homes in Hudson to Temple Israel of Catskill for Yom Kippur evening services. From the moment that Rabbi Zoe entered the synagogue chanting Kol Nidre in her smooth tenor voice, we were hooked and felt our ancestors rumbling around ourselves. Charlotte, my friend and agent, said, "We have to meet the rabbi." So, we did. A week later, we had arranged a lunch with her in Hudson and scoped out a version of this book. The version never veered from our original idea.

Iraqi Jews include a dish called *seudah mafseket*, which means "separating meal" or "dish of cessation," the evening before the fast. It could be a stuffed chicken slowly cooked in rice. In Morocco, an Erev Yom Kippur meal might be their well-known tomato soup called *harira*, which can be loaded with lentils or chickpeas, plus fragrant herbs and spices.

Challah

DOUGH

¾ cup warm water

1 packet (2¼ teaspoons) active dry yeast

1 tablespoon sugar

5 tablespoons vegetable oil, plus more for bowl

2 large eggs, at room temperature

1 large egg yolk, at room temperature

4 cups all-purpose flour, plus more if needed and for dusting

2 teaspoons coarse kosher salt

EGG WASH

1 large egg whisked with a pinch of salt

OPTIONAL TOPPINGS

Toasted sesame seeds

Poppy seeds

Flaky sea salt

Fennel seeds

Or everything

There are many, many recipes out there for challah. There are also places to purchase one. In fact, bakeries all over the country are beginning to bake challah for Friday evening Shabbat dinners. To paraphrase a well-known advertisement, "You don't have to be Jewish to love challah."

My friend Roy put together this challah recipe for me. The simple, three-strand braid makes a large crumb loaf—just the right size for making Elvis's beloved sandwich.

1. Make the dough: Combine the water, yeast, and sugar in the bowl of a stand mixer fitted with the paddle attachment. Stir. Let it stand until frothy, about 5 minutes.

2. Add the oil, honey, eggs, and egg yolk and beat with the paddle until mixed. Add 3 cups of the flour and beat until combined.

3. Switch to the dough hook—make sure to scrape everything off the paddle and back into the bowl—and add the remaining cup of flour and the salt. Mix on low speed to incorporate the flour. Then, increase the speed to just below medium and knead until silky smooth, about 7 minutes. About halfway through, stop the machine and check the dough. It should feel moist but not sticky. If you need to, add more flour by the tablespoon.

4. Turn out the dough onto a lightly floured surface and knead for a minute or so. Pull off a small piece of dough and stretch it. It should become thin enough in the center to see light through. If not, keep kneading. Form the dough into a ball.

5. Oil a bowl generously with vegetable oil. Add the ball of dough, then turn the dough over to oil all sides of it. Cover the dough with plastic wrap and a clean kitchen towel and move the bowl to a warm spot. Leave the dough to rise until doubled in volume, 1½ to 2 hours. If the day is cool, it will likely take longer.

6. Turn out the dough onto a lightly floured surface and knead it for about a minute. Divide the dough into thirds and roll each piece into a 20-inch rope with tapering ends. Line them up next to one another, then, starting from one end of the three ropes, pinch together those three ends and braid the ropes. (Lift the center rope and slide the right rope under it. Lift the new center rope and slide the left under it. Repeat to the end, keeping the braid gently snug.) Pinch together the three ends at the far end.

7. Gently transfer the loaf to a large, parchment paper-lined baking sheet. Tuck under the pinched ends of the loaf to make an even shape. Cover with a clean kitchen towel, move the pan to a warm place, and leave the loaf to rise until doubled in volume, about 1 hour.

8. Halfway through the rising time, heat the oven to 350°F.

9. Brush the loaf gently with the egg wash and sprinkle with any toppings. For the Elvis sandwich, I leave it plain and let the fillings star.

10. Bake until the loaf is a rich golden brown and the interior temperature reads 190°F on an instant-read thermometer, 25 to 30 minutes.

11. Remove from the oven and let cool for at least an hour before slicing.

12. This is best the day it's baked, but you can store leftovers in a plastic bag with all the air squeezed out, or wrapped in plastic wrap.

13. Use a serrated knife to cut into slices.

Elvis Presley's Fried Peanut Butter and Banana Sandwiches

SERVES 1

2 slices Challah (page 54)

1 medium ripe banana

2 tablespoons chunky peanut butter

2 tablespoons unsalted butter

Talk about food that will stick to your ribs and power you through 25 hours of contemplation. Here's the sandwich for you. Roselle Chartock writes about Rabbi Alfred Fruchter and his wife, Jeannette, who were the Presleys' upstairs neighbors in a large Victorian house in Memphis. "Jeannette . . . explained how, once a month, they would have the Presleys over for Friday Sabbath dinner. 'Elvis loved our food,' she said, 'especially the challah. He would have his peanut butter and banana sandwich, his favorite food, on challah.'" He was also the Fruchters' *Shabbos goy*—a non-Jew hired by Jews to perform certain chores for them that they are prohibited from doing on the Sabbath.

1. Lightly toast the challah (to keep it from ripping when the peanut butter is spread on it).

2. Mash the banana on one slice of challah, then spread the peanut butter on the other slice. Close the spread sides together.

3. Melt the butter in a small skillet over medium heat, then fry the sandwich on each side until both sides are golden brown.

4. It's most easily consumed if cut on the diagonal to serve.

Roselle Chartock, in her infinitely interesting book *The Jewish World of Elvis Presley*, quotes one of Elvis's costars from his movie *Girl Happy*, Joby Baker: "'One day . . . Elvis mentioned how much he loved chitlins.'" . . . Joby thought Elvis would like *gribenes* (scraps of fried chicken or goose cracklings and onion) . . . Joby made some for Elvis, who loved the dish. Joby said, 'Elvis used to ask me [in Yiddish] to make gribenes. *Esppes schtickel gribenes? . . .* It was his favorite food besides fried peanut butter and banana sandwiches.'"

Roasted Cauliflower Salad
with Dates, Pecans, and Fried Shallots

SERVES 4 TO 6

1 head cauliflower (about 1½ pounds), cut into medium florets (they'll shrink a bit when roasted)

1 tablespoon date syrup

3 tablespoons olive oil

1 teaspoon salt, plus more as needed

3 large Medjool dates, pitted and chopped

¼ cup pan-toasted pecans, chopped

½ teaspoon rose harissa

½ cup sliced shallots

The ingredients in this salad play together so well. You'd almost think they were best friends. I've used dates in two ways, as a syrup drenched into the cauliflower florets to roast, and chopped up in the finished salad. The last-minute fried shallots add a nice crunch to the salad. There are many references to dates in the Bible—and you'll learn about them when you make your way to Chapter 9, which concerns Tu B'Shevat, a holiday that celebrates the Seven Species of plants mentioned in the Bible. View this recipe as a coming attraction.

1. Heat the oven to 350°F.

2. Line a rimmed baking sheet with parchment paper. Arrange the cauliflower florets in a single layer on the parchment. Add the date syrup, 1 tablespoon of the olive oil, and the teaspoon of salt. Use your hands to thoroughly coat the florets and return them to a single layer. Roast in the oven, occasionally tossing the florets, for about 45 minutes. You want them to be slightly golden on all sides. They don't need to be crisp; al dente is OK. Remove the pan from the oven and let cool.

3. Transfer the cauliflower to a bowl. Add the Medjool dates, pecans, rose harissa, 1 tablespoon of the remaining tablespoon olive oil, and salt to taste. Toss together and set aside.

4. Heat the remaining tablespoon of olive oil in a small skillet over medium heat. When the oil is warm, add the shallots. Stir them around the oil until they're deep gold and appear to be crispy. Immediately remove from the heat and add them to the cauliflower to prevent them from burning. Toss to combine. Taste once more for salt and add as desired.

5. Serve at room temperature.

57

Olive Oil–Roasted Pears, Labna, Date Pudding

What better way to staunch your appetite than with a serving of fruit, cheese, and bread. The date pudding is a chewy square jammed-filled with dates and walnuts that will make a good substitute for bread—any day.

SERVES 6 TO 8

PEARS

6 Bosc or Anjou pears

2 tablespoons olive oil

DATE PUDDING

1½ cups coarsely chopped dates

1 cup coarsely chopped walnuts

3 rounded tablespoons all-purpose flour

½ cup sugar

1 teaspoon baking powder

1 tablespoon unsalted butter, melted, plus more for pan

2 large eggs, lightly beaten

Labna (page 25)

MAKE THE PEARS

1. Heat the oven to 375°F.

2. Quarter the pears. Remove the stem and cut each quarter into three or four slices.

3. Place the pears on a parchment paper-lined rimmed baking sheet. Pour the olive oil over them and use your hands to thoroughly coat the pears.

4. Roast in the oven, turning from time to time, until the pears are deep gold and slightly shrunken, about 45 minutes.

5. Remove from the oven and let cool to serve.

MAKE THE DATE PUDDING

1. Combine the dates, walnuts, flour, sugar, baking powder, melted butter, and eggs in a medium bowl and stir until thoroughly blended.

2. Generously butter an 8-inch square baking pan. Pour the batter into the pan. Use a rubber spatula to evenly distribute the batter. Bake for 30 minutes, or until a tester inserted into the center comes out clean.

3. Remove from the oven and let cool on a wire rack. Cut into sixteen 2-inch squares. Store in an airtight container for up to 2 weeks. These freeze perfectly.

TO SERVE

1. Place a date square, some pears, and labna on a plate. Alternatively, pile the date squares on a plate, the pears in a bowl, and the labna in another bowl and let people serve themselves.

Gravlax

SERVES 16

1 tablespoon crushed white peppercorns (use a mortar and pestle)

¼ cup kosher salt

2 tablespoons honey

2 tablespoons Swedish aquavit (akvavit) that contains caraway or dill, and fennel

One 2½-pound center-cut salmon fillet, skin on

18 to 20 dill sprigs

New York Jewish delis will tell you that one of their busiest days of the year is the day before Yom Kippur, when Jews line up and then load up on everything they need to break their fast. Bags will be filled with whitefish salad, paper-thin slices of sable, all kinds of herring from marinated to enrobed in cream sauce, three different kinds of cream cheese, potato salad, coleslaw, bagels, rye bread, pastries—and lox. Why not make this Scandinavian cured salmon preparation, gravlax, and enjoy the satisfaction of making something by yourself. The gravlax needs several days to cure, so it can be made several days before you need to stop and atone. Serve with the bread and sauces of your choice. I choose dark bread, and a quick sauce made with Dijon mustard, crème fraîche, and more chopped dill.

1. Prepare the salmon: Combine the crushed peppercorns, salt, honey, and aquavit in a small bowl and stir well. Cut the salmon in half crosswise. Place one half, skin side down, in a glass or ceramic baking dish. Completely saturate the fish with the peppercorn mixture and cover it with piles of dill. Place the other salmon fillet over it, skin side up.

2. Loosely cover the baking dish with plastic wrap and weigh down the entire surface of the fish with heavy objects, such as a cast-iron skillet or can of tomatoes. Place in the refrigerator.

3. After 12 hours, remove from the refrigerator, unwrap, and turn the fish over. Separate the fillets and spoon the liquid that has begun to fill the baking dish over the two halves. Put the fillets together again. Re-cover with plastic wrap and weigh down the fish again. Refrigerate for another 48 hours, repeating the turning and spooning every 12 hours. Serve thinly sliced on the diagonal, or keep refrigerated for up to 2 weeks.

Coleslaw *with Poppy Seeds*

SERVES 10 TO 12

1 pound red cabbage, cored
and shredded finely

1 pound green cabbage,
cored and shredded finely

1 pound carrots, peeled and
shredded finely

1 small onion, grated

1 cup good-quality
mayonnaise

1 garlic clove, mashed
through a press

Grated zest and juice of
1 orange

2 tablespoons poppy seeds

2 tablespoons white vinegar

2 teaspoons salt

Freshly ground white pepper

The origins of coleslaw are up for discussion. This shredded cabbage salad may have first been made in a rudimentary way when the Romans served a dish of cabbage with vinegar and spices. With its name, *koosla* (cabbage salad), it was probably brought to our shores by the Dutch when they landed in New York.

My mother made the best coleslaw. She used onion and garlic powders to season her slaw. I've re-created her dish using fresh onion and garlic. This slaw gets better and better the longer it marinates, making it just the right make-ahead dish for breaking your fast.

1. Combine the red and green cabbage, carrots, and onion in a large bowl. Toss to mix well.

2. Whisk together the mayonnaise, garlic, orange zest and juice, poppy seeds, vinegar, salt, and white pepper to taste in a small bowl. Add the dressing to the vegetables and mix well. Chill. Bring to room temperature before serving.

3. This salad gets better as it marinates. It will keep for up to a week in the refrigerator.

Pickled vegetables in any form are found on Jewish menus all over the world. It's a time-honored way to preserve vegetables. Do you remember the bowls of pickled cucumbers and tomatoes (there's a pickled cherry tomato recipe on page 213) set in place at a Jewish deli, gratis for the diner, that you gobbled up before your pastrami sandwich accompanied by a little paper container of coleslaw arrived? Coleslaw is a cabbage salad trying to trick you into eating more pickles. This is especially true when it's made ahead to serve at a Yom Kippur break fast and has the opportunity to get a nice little fermentation going on.

Noodle Kugel *with Apples and Raisins, Walnut Crumble*

SERVES 10 TO 12

TOPPING

1 cup packed dark brown sugar

¾ cup all-purpose flour

¾ cup coarsely chopped walnuts

2 teaspoons ground cinnamon

¼ teaspoon salt

8 tablespoons (1 stick) unsalted butter cut in ½-inch pieces, plus more for pan

KUGEL

One 12-ounce bag wide egg noodles

5 large eggs

1 cup large-curd cottage cheese

1½ cups heavy cream

¼ cup granulated sugar

1 teaspoon salt

1 large apple peeled, cored, and small diced (about 1¼ cups)

½ cup raisins

2 tablespoons finely chopped crystallized ginger

Now, here's a dish that's probably stored in every Jewish person's secular or religious memory bank. It can be mentioned with great joy—or fear of what's about to appear on the table. It seems that grandmas always made the sometimes controversial kugels—an often stodgy sweet or savory pudding made with noodles or potatoes. I choose noodles, and a sweet version. For this *lokshen* (noodle) kugel, I decided to up the game and add apples, raisins, and candied ginger to the base, and make it even sweeter with a walnut crumble topping.

MAKE THE TOPPING

1. Combine the brown sugar, flour, walnuts, cinnamon, and salt in a medium bowl. Use your fingers to thoroughly mix the ingredients. Add the butter pieces and rub them together with the dry ingredients until a crumbly texture is achieved. Keep cool until ready to use.

MAKE THE KUGEL

1. Heat the oven to 350°F. Butter a 9-by-13-inch baking or a gratin dish of similar size.

2. Cook the noodles in abundant boiling, salted water for about 4 minutes. Drain.

3. Whisk together the eggs, cottage cheese, cream, granulated sugar, and salt in a large bowl. Add the noodles, apple, raisins, and ginger. Toss together to thoroughly combine. Transfer the mixture to the prepared baking dish.

4. Evenly cover the kugel with the crumble topping. Bake until the sides are bubbly and the topping is set, 45 minutes to 1 hour.

5. Serve warm or at room temperature. It's delicious the next day for breakfast.

CHAPTER FOUR

Sukkot

*The moon
bursting with her fullness sings,
"Let everything that has breath
praise Yah!"[26]*

From the Rabbi

Susan: *Because Sukkot comes at harvest time, does it have a special meaning?*

Zoe: This is the first of five full-moon holidays in our yearly calendar, all occurring on the 15th of their respective Hebrew months. From the 15th to 21st of Tishrei, we celebrate the weeklong harvest moon festival of Sukkot. Following immediately on its heels are the holidays of Shemini Atzeret and Simchat Torah.

Sukkot is a glorious invitation to spend as much time as possible in nature and dwell in a sukkah—a temporary dwelling we build at this time of year. After all the time spent in self-examination and contemplation throughout the month of Elul, Rosh HaShanah, and Yom Kippur, this festival is the reward that follows. "Sukkot" is the plural of *sukkah* (booth or shelter). In the Torah, the Holy One spoke, saying, "So that your descendants will know that I made the Israelites live in sukkot—temporary shelters, when I brought them out of the land of Egypt, I am Adonai your God."[27] The sukkah also symbolizes The Clouds of Glory that appeared when the Israelites first left the land of Egypt after having been freed by The Hand of God from slavery. These mysterious, perhaps mystical, clouds protected them during the 40 years as they journeyed in the desert to the Promised Land. Time in the sukkah offers us sacred time to reflect on how our ancestors were protected and be grateful for the many ways that we, too,

---

26   Psalm 150:6
27   Leviticus 23:43

are protected and provided for. We marvel at the fragility of life highlighted in the Book of Ecclesiastes that we read on this festival. Each experience we have with building and or decorating a sukkah, preparing, or serving a meal, inviting guests, remembering our ancestors, shaking the *lulav* (date tree frond) and *etrog* (citron), praying for rain, marching in a tuneful processional around the synagogue, and let's not leave out sleeping in the sukkah, all allow us myriad opportunities to find the joy in Sukkot.

I can't think of a more appropriate and joyous place to celebrate the holiday than here, in the fertile Hudson Valley. What's so unique about Temple Israel of Catskill's festival?

The tradition is to begin building the sukkah immediately after Yom Kippur, but in our community, we start six months earlier in the springtime, just after Passover, when the threat of frost is completely behind us. A sukkah is a temporary shelter, but we have a slender metal frame that stays up all year-round, which is not the custom but makes the next steps possible. We plant corn at each of the corners and several kinds of unusual gourd seeds all around the base of the frame. I recommend the more unusually shaped ones, such as gooseneck, apple, or pear, although I never met a gourd I didn't love. One year, a congregant planted a tiny hops plant by one of the poles and now we have a monster of a plant that produces generous handfuls of glorious hops that make for an exotic look. A couple dug up some bamboo from their land and transplanted it at the temple. Every year, congregants continue to expand our garden beds with flowers and strongly scented herbs for our Havdalah Garden. Havdalah (separation) is the ritual that ends Shabbat. When the gourds begin growing, we run strings vertically up the sides of the sukkah so that they have an enticing jungle gym to climb upon. This is how we plan for the magnificent harvest festival of Sukkot.

All summer, we cultivate the plants on our temple grounds. Just before Sukkot, we invite our community to bring herbs and flowers from their gardens, tying strings around bunches of absolutely everything we can find. We invite the community and fill the sukkah with bales of hay, gourds, pumpkins, and colorful Flint corn. Baskets of baby gourds and small bunches of flowers and herbs are all tied with strings and placed just outside the sukkah, so that everyone can

The etrog is shaped like a heart; the lulav, the spine; the myrtle leaves, like eyes; and the willow leaves, like lips. This reminds us to be mindful of where we direct our heart, where we focus our attention, and what words we choose to say. It is a reminder to use the gifts of our body wisely.

share in the joy of hanging something on the sukkah. We cut down the bamboo and toss each feathered lengthy stalk, arching it high in the air with a javelin throw to populate our sukkah roof, creating a lush *sechach* (the covering of the sukkah created from harvested materials) with its splendor.

Sukkot being a harvest festival, the sukkah must be made only from what was harvested, not of living things. Ours has living plants growing up it all summer and fall, but just before the festival, I take my clippers and cut everything from the base of the plants, making sure not to leave one root connected to a plant. Now, we have a kosher sukkah and one we can't wait to share with the entire community. Each year's sukkah is different from the previous one, and each time, I'm filled with awe of the temporary shelter we create so that we might give thanks to the One who provides our bounty.

Does Sukkot have more than one name?

Yes, and each name gives us insight into different aspects of this multilayered festival. Torah describes Sukkot as Chag Haasif (Festival of Gathering).[28] This refers to the time when farmers in Israel would gather up their crops that had been drying in their fields. Because Sukkot is supposed to be the most joyous of the three festivals that include Pesach and Shavuot, our sages simply called it Chag (festival). It is like saying Sukkot is the festival of festivals. In our liturgy, Sukkot is also referred to as Zeman Simchatenu (The Time of Our Rejoicing). Our festivals and many holidays have multiple names reflecting both the evolution of that holiday and our traditions' generosity, offering us many avenues of access.

I know it is customary to invite guests into the sukkah, but I heard you also invite those who have passed. Is this really something you do?

Our sages teach that "hospitality toward guests is greater than receiving the Divine Presence!"[29] It is a mitzvah to open our homes to others as Abraham modeled for us in Torah. The Divine was visiting him when he looked up and saw three strangers off in the distance. Abraham basically asked God to wait while he dashed out to welcome them into his humble tent. He was 99 years young, in pain and healing from his *brit milah* (Covenant of Circumcision) that had taken place the previous day.

It is said that to fully realize Sukkot, our sukkah must include "you, your sons, your daughters, your servants, your maids and the strangers within your

---

28 Exodus 23:16
29 Talmud Shabbat 127a

gates."[30] This picture that Torah paints for us is quite specific. It is pure joy, connection to nature, ourselves, and one another. What better time to spread the joy.

We have a fascinating tradition of extending our guest list to seven supernal guests: Abraham, Isaac, Jacob, Moses, Aaron, Joseph, and David, our founding fathers. For each of the seven days, we focus on one guest and their qualities hoping to be imbued with their attributes. These guests are called Ushpizin—"guests" in Aramaic. I find this Kabbalistic custom to be fascinating. Like many, I include our founding mothers, and have extended the whole concept to inviting those who have passed in my personal life into the sukkah. How marvelous it is to set aside time like this to be in nature, away from our daily distractions, and to allow ourselves to feel close to our loved ones who have passed. We can think about their wonderful qualities and how to cultivate them within ourselves. The fact that Sukkot creates time and space for this is beyond precious to me. Who will you be inviting into your sukkah this year?

Are there other rituals that are specific to Sukkot?
We have a unique mitzvah reserved for Sukkot and everything we need to fulfill it comes from the earth. The Torah instructs us to gather Arba'ah Minim[31]—the four species consisting of lulav (palm), *aravot* (willow), *hadassim* (myrtle), and the star of the ritual, etrog (the exotic, aromatic citron fruit). The first three species, when wrapped together with palm leaves, are also referred to as lulav. The ritual we do with these items is primal and engages our whole body. Every day during Sukkot, except for Shabbat, while holding the lulav and etrog, we wave them in all six directions—south, north, east, up, down, and west, giving thanks to the One who provides life from every direction. Kabbalist Rabbi Isaac Luria, also called the Arizal, taught that after shaking them in each direction, we are to bring them to our hearts. When I teach our L'Hadlik Hebrew School students, I pause after bringing the lulav and etrog to my heart and invite everyone to call out what they are giving thanks for that comes from that particular direction. It may be home, where a friend lives, or our favorite ice cream store. It might be snow from the skies, blueberries from the earth, or Grandma who lives in the South. This is a spontaneous way to pray together, whether with children or adults, that always brings about unexpected responses.

There are many thought-provoking explanations of the symbolism of the four species. The sages teach that each corresponds to a body part: the etrog is shaped like a heart; the lulav, the spine; the myrtle leaves, like eyes; and the

---

30   Deuteronomy 16:14
31   Leviticus 23:40

willow leaves, like lips.[32] This reminds us to be mindful of where we direct our heart, where we focus our attention, and what words we choose to say. It is a reminder to use the gifts of our body wisely.

Another wonderful teaching is based on the four different trees that produce the four species and the symbolism of their respective qualities. The etrog has both taste and scent. The date palm, the lulav, only has taste; the myrtle, only scent; and the willow has neither taste nor scent.[33] The sages teach that this is representative of the different types of Jews. What one lacks, the other makes up for. We need one another and are better and stronger together.

My personal and synagogue community is made up of a diverse group of people, many of whom come from other faith traditions. For me, it is organic to extend this teaching to include all people. Rabbi Jonathan Sacks, of blessed memory, described what I feel in my heart with such precision:

Humanity is formed out of our commonalities and differences. Our differences shape our identity. Our commonalities form our humanity. We are neither completely different, nor all the same. If we were completely different, we could not communicate. If we were all alike, we would have nothing to say. Our differences matter. But so too does the truth that despite our religious differences, we share a common humanity. Sukkot is thus the festival of a double joy: at being part of this people, yet also participating in the universal fate of humankind. [34]

May shaking the lulav and etrog help to shake us up in the ways we need shaking up, so that when the shaking ends, we may find ourselves dwelling in the calm of sukkat *shlomecha*[35] (a shelter of peace).

32   Midrash Rabba 30:14
33   Midrash Leviticus Rabba 30:12
34   *Ceremony & Celebration*, Rabbi Jonathan Sacks (Maggid Books & OU Press; 2017), p. 110.
35   This phrase is found in Hashkivenu, a prayer from the Maariv (evening prayer service), as well as part of the bedtime Sh'ma. See *The Koren Siddur* (Koren Publishers Jerusalem: 2009), pp. 250 and 297e.

From the Cook

My most vivid memories of Sukkot are of driving through the Williamsburg and Crown Heights sections of Brooklyn, New York, and seeing the balconies of apartment buildings turned into sukkahs. The outdoor spaces were adorned with swathes of greens, bunches of brightly colored flint corn, and dangling gourds, enclosed with a neutral-colored canvas curtain to ensure privacy. My most recent experience with a sukkah was the one constructed on Temple Israel of Catskill's property. Members of the congregation grew extra produce in their gardens to help decorate the sukkah, adding brightly colored and personal touches to it.

Any food that includes the food of your area's harvest works for this chapter. Askenazi Jews might include tzimmes, a dish made with carrots, raisins, and other root vegetables, on their holiday tables. The Jews of North African and Middle Eastern countries might bring to the table a huge mound of couscous covered with stewed vegetables.

Ushpizin is the title of a Israeli film that portrays the invited supernal sukkah guests—ushpizin—as con men adding levity to an already spirited holiday.

Arrope

MAKES APPROXIMATELY 3 PINTS

3 quarts Concord grapes

5 semidried figs

3½ cups peeled and seeded butternut squash cut in 2-inch chunks

2 quarts water

Arrope is a syrup made with raisins, for Passover, by the Sephardic Jews of the Iberian Peninsula. The syrup is not exclusive to the Jewish population. In Spain, you can find makers who put it together with grapes, sweetened with figs and sometimes, as in this recipe, with squash. I call for it as a topping on Masa Tiganitas (page 164) for Passover. Use it when you can make it with the fall harvest, and then as an addition to a dressing for bitter greens, drizzled over a log of fresh goat cheese, or to add depth and fragrance to a sauce. Freeze some to thaw for Passover.

I used a 6-quart copper jam pot to make the arrope.

1. Combine the grapes, figs, squash, and water in a copper jam pot or stockpot over medium heat. Cook until the squash is just about tender, 30 to 40 minutes. Remove from the heat and let cool. It will continue to cook as it cools.

2. Pass the mixture through a fine-mesh sieve. (You may have to push a bit harder because of the figs.)

3. Transfer the syrup into jars–it will keep for up to 2 weeks, refrigerated–or into lidded plastic containers for the freezer.

Pumpkin Soup *with Apples and Cinnamon Croutons*

MAKES 1½ QUARTS

APPLE GARNISH

1 sweet, crisp apple (I use Gala), quartered, cored, peeled, and cut into ¼-inch dice

1 tablespoon freshly squeezed lemon juice

SOUP

One 2¼-pound squash (I use butternut), peeled, seeded, and cut into 2-inch chunks (about 5 cups)

1 large, crisp, sweet apple (I use Gala), skin-on, quartered, cored, and cut into 1-inch chunks

1 medium yellow onion, chopped coarsely

5 or 6 fresh sage leaves

¼ cup olive oil

1 quart vegetable stock

1 teaspoon rose harissa,

½ teaspoon freshly ground white pepper, or ½ teaspoon Aleppo pepper flakes

CINNAMON CROUTONS

2 tablespoons unsalted butter

Five ½-inch-thick slices Challah (page 54) or pain de mie, cut into ½-inch squares

1 teaspoon ground cinnamon

¼ teaspoon salt

The fall harvest is the headliner for this chapter, and nothing is more emblematic of the harvest than all forms of hard-skinned squash. I call this soup "pumpkin" after the most famous of cold-weather squash, and its history with the Jews. It was brought back from the Americas by Spanish explorers and became a favorite ingredient in the food of the Jews who viewed it as a food of thanksgiving. Imagine that.

However, I use butternut squash for this soup because it's the easiest to peel. Any squash with hard skin and deep orange flesh will work. The somewhat sweet soup wouldn't mind some additional spice, such as Aleppo pepper flakes, or rose harissa. I'll leave it up to you.

1. Make the apple garnish: Place the diced apple in a bowl and toss with the lemon juice. Set aside.

2. Make the soup: Heat the oven to 400°F.

3. Place the squash, apples, onion, and sage on a parchment paper–lined rimmed baking sheet. Pour in the olive oil and toss the ingredients together to evenly coat.

4. Roast in the oven, turning the vegetables once or twice, until they're golden and the squash is fork-tender, about 30 minutes. Remove from the oven and lower the heat to 300°F.

5. Transfer the cooked vegetables to a large pot over medium-low heat. Add the vegetable stock. Add the rose harissa, white pepper, or Aleppo pepper flakes. Simmer for 15 minutes. Remove from the heat. Let cool. Use an immersion blender to blend the soup until smooth.

6. While the soup is simmering, make the croutons: Place the butter on a rimmed baking sheet and put into the oven. When the butter has melted, remove the pan from the oven and add the diced bread, cinnamon, and salt to the butter. Thoroughly combine the ingredients to evenly coat the bread. Put back in the oven and toast, flipping the croutons once or twice, until they appear golden and crunchy, about 15 minutes. Remove from the oven.

7. To serve: Add the hot/warm soup to bowls. Garnish with cinnamon croutons and diced apple.

NOTES: *You may want to add salt—I don't, as I use commercially prepared organic vegetable broth, which I find to be adequately salted.*

Add more seasoning as desired. This soup is thick—you may want to thin it with a bit more broth.

Fresh Corn Mamaliga

SERVES 12

¼ cup olive oil, plus
  2 teaspoons for bowl

7 cups water

1 teaspoon salt

2 cups instant polenta

2 cups fresh corn kernels
  (from 2 ears)

I was surprised to hear how many people, Jews or Jewish associated, were familiar with *mamaliga* when I mentioned that I was going to include a version of it in this book (a friend even spoke about its being a quasi-naughty expression when he was a 12-year-old). Mamaliga, originally a Romanian dish, is essentially polenta. Cornmeal grits. Most people who were aware of mamaliga talked about the vast amounts of sour cream, butter, and cheeses that were added to the cornmeal. The Moldovan version is garnished with fried lardoons. Oy. None of these versions would do for this book.

I wanted a mamaliga that would serve as a side dish to meat or poultry dishes—therefore, no competing dairy ingredients allowed. I love making polenta with fresh corn kernels to which I usually adding grated Parmesan. How about eliminating the cheese and add just fresh corn, olive oil, and salt. Yup. That works. And, when you pour the cooked mamaliga into an oiled bowl, let it cool, and then turn out the dome onto a plate. Wow—what a great presentation. This recipe makes vast amounts of mamaliga. On purpose—because the leftovers can be made into good things, too.

1. Use 2 teaspoons of olive oil to oil a medium glass or ceramic bowl.

2. Combine the water and salt in large pot, such as a stockpot, over medium-high heat. When the water boils, slowly pour the polenta into it, whisking it the whole time to prevent lumps. When the polenta is fully incorporated into the water, you can switch to a wooden spoon to continue stirring. You will need to stir the mamaliga for longer than most package directions suggest, as I've added more water than they do. More water and more stirring ensure a smooth, well-cooked mamaliga.

3. When the polenta begins to bubble and erupt, lower
    the heat to low and add the corn kernels and the ¼ cup
    of olive oil. Continue to stir until a thick mixture is
    achieved. Carefully pour the polenta into the oiled bowl.
    Let cool. Run a knife around the edge of the bowl and
    invert the mamaliga onto a serving platter. Slice into
    wedges to serve.

4. Mamaliga leftovers can be fried in oil or butter—be aware
    that the corn kernels may pop onto you—and served with
    scrambled eggs, chopped salad, or topped with butter
    and Amarene (page 197), Arrope (page 69), and so on.
    Grill the slices when you're grilling burgers or chicken—
    remember, the mamaliga is pareve, so it can be eaten
    with meat.

Chickpea Sambusaks

My spicy chickpea filling is offset by salty feta that's nested inside simple pastry, folded, sealed, and then showered with sesame seeds. I use a simple, tight dough to make the sambusaks; however, they can be made with phyllo dough or puff pastry as well.

MAKES 20 TO 22 SAMBUSAKS

DOUGH

3 cups all-purpose flour, plus more for dusting

1 teaspoon salt

8 tablespoons (1 stick) unsalted butter, at room temperature

½ cup cold water or drained chickpea liquid

⅓ cup olive oil

1 large egg, beaten, for glaze

Sesame seeds

FILLING

Two 15-ounce cans chickpeas, drained and rinsed

¼ cup olive oil

¾ cup finely chopped onion

1 garlic clove, chopped finely

1 tablespoon salt

1 heaping teaspoon lemon zest

2 teaspoons fresh thyme leaves

½ teaspoon Aleppo pepper flakes

¾ cup crumbled feta

Optional dip: Labna (page 25) mixed with *amba*, a delicious Iraqi spicy mango sauce that you can locate from the usual online sources

1. Make the dough: Combine the flour and salt in a large bowl. Cream the butter and add to the flour mixture. Add the water or chickpea water and the olive oil. Mix well.

2. Knead the dough until it forms a ball. Prepare to work it for a few minutes—it will be tight.

3. Cover the dough and set aside.

4. Make the filling: Place the chickpeas in a food processor and process until they resemble chunky peanut butter. Transfer to a medium bowl.

5. Heat the olive oil in a large skillet or shallow saucepan over medium heat. Add the onion and garlic. Sauté until the onion is translucent, 2 to 3 minutes.

6. Add the chopped chickpeas, salt, lemon zest, thyme, and Aleppo pepper flakes. Toss together to combine. Cook for about 3 minutes. Remove from the heat and place back into the chickpea bowl. Add the feta and stir.

7. Heat the oven to 350°F.

8. Make the sambusaks: Divide the ball of dough in half. Place one portion on a floured work surface and roll out as thinly as possible, even less than ¼ inch. Use a 3-inch biscuit cutter to cut circles. Roll out each circle to make the dough even thinner. Line up the circles on a parchment paper–lined baking sheet. Place a generous tablespoon of the chickpea filling off-center on each circle. Fold over the dough to make a half-moon. Use the tines of a fork to crimp and seal the sambusak.

9. Repeat the process with all the remaining dough—including the scraps, which can be gathered together and rolled again.

10. Use a pastry brush to glaze each sambusak. Shower copious (my choice) amounts of sesame seeds over the top. Bake until golden brown, about 30 minutes.

11. Serve hot or at room temperature with a dip of your choice—or not.

Sambusaks can be called samosas, or *bourekas*, even empanadas, and they're still the same—filled with cheese, meat, or vegetables—turnovers, baked or fried, depending on where in the world they're made, and who's making them. These additive little pastries are often used to celebrate the holidays of all the world's major religions. Sambusaks, stuffed with chickpeas—one of the most ancient legumes, and one used in Jewish food all over the world—are usually credited to the Mizrahi Jews of Iraq, who may use them as a Shabbat snack.

Spicy, Sweet, and Sour Braised Venison

SERVES 6

1¾ to 2 pounds butterflied leg of fallow deer, or same amount bottom round

2 cups red wine

1 cup pomegranate molasses

3 cups thinly sliced yellow onions

2 celery stalks, cut on the diagonal (1 to 1½ cups)

1 cup sliced carrots, cut on the diagonal

¼ cup olive oil

2 tablespoons tomato paste

2 tablespoons date syrup

2 teaspoons dried thyme leaves

1 teaspoon Aleppo pepper flakes, or more to taste

2 teaspoons salt

At the last minute of making recipe entries, I did an about-face and changed a beef brisket–an every-Ashkenazi-Jewish-holiday favorite dish recipe that I was planning–to this one that uses venison instead. Tikkun Olam was on my mind. Low-fat venison wants flavor and oil added to it. I like the way the mix of North African ingredients endorses the braise and gives it a dense and rich sauce. Serve with Mamaliga (page 72), rice, or olive oil–mashed potatoes.

1. Cut the butterflied leg of venison into four as-equal-as-possible pieces. Place them in a large bowl. Add the wine, pomegranate molasses, onions, celery, and carrots. Cover and refrigerate overnight.

2. Heat the oven to 300°F. Remove the marinated venison from the refrigerator. Bring to room temperature.

3. Transfer the venison with the wine and vegetable mixture to a Dutch oven. Add the olive oil, tomato paste, date syrup, thyme, Aleppo pepper flakes, and salt. Toss to combine the ingredients. Cover and slide into the oven.

4. Roast in the oven, tossing a few times while cooking, until fork-tender, 2 to 3 hours.

5. If the sauce still seems a bit loose, place the Dutch oven over medium-low heat and reduce the sauce to a thick consistency.

6. Slice the venison against the grain. Serve covered in sauce, with side dishes of your choice.

Tikkun Olam is a concept in Judaism that references the broken aspects of the universe and talks about how to repair them—make them whole. For example, if you eat meat, you might consider wild or farm game, such as venison, as an alternative to other red meats, such as beef or lamb. Not only is the lean flesh from the deer heart-healthy, with its high protein and low cholesterol content, but eating deer is more environmentally friendly than beef. Deer, either locally hunted in the wild, or raised on farms, means there's a low carbon footprint not only from animal methane emissions but also from greenhouse gas emissions from long-haul transportation that brings other red meats to nationwide markets. Ecologically speaking, changing your diet to respect your own body and, at the same time, considering the health of the planet you inhabit is a kind of Tikkun Olam.

Passion Fruit Curd

MAKES ABOUT 2 CUPS

4 large egg yolks

1 large egg

1 cup sugar

⅔ cup passion fruit pulp

8 tablespoons (1 stick)
    unsalted butter

½ teaspoon salt

I have a friend in California who sends me the most marvelous produce from his ever-blooming garden—including passion fruit, when he harvests it sometime in early autumn. When I thought about what would be in this book, I knew that I had to include recipes made with West Coast produce (I know I'm a bit East Coast-centric). Passion fruit, with its surreally beautiful blossoms and its odd leathery skin that gets wrinkled to let you know that it's ripe, and its even odder pulp full of black seeds, has flavor like nothing you've ever tasted—tart, sweet, and floral. The good thing about the pulp is that it's easy to freeze, and then to pull out to make this curd any time of the year—or make juice to use as the base of a fine salad dressing or an essential cocktail mix. I use some passion fruit to make this curd as soon as they're ripe. I scoop out the pulp from the remaining fruit, put it into containers clearly marked with amounts, then freeze it to make more curd for Cornmeal Shortcakes with Passion Fruit Curd and Blackberry and Blueberry Sauce (page 219) for Tu B'Av.

1. Whisk together the yolks, egg, and sugar in a medium bowl.

2. Heat the passion fruit pulp and butter together in a heavy-bottomed, nonreactive saucepan over low heat.

3. Remove from the heat and whisk a bit of the passion fruit mixture into the egg mixture. Keep whisking as you continue to add the fruit mixture to the egg mixture.

4. Pour the entire mixture back into the saucepan over medium heat. Use a silicone spatula to continue to stir, scraping the bottom and sides of the pot until the mixture completely coats the spatula, 6 to 10 minutes.

5. Remove from the heat and strain through a fine-mesh strainer into a ceramic bowl. Cover with plastic wrap directly on the surface of the curd. Chill until further thickened and cooled, about 2 hours.

6. Place in a glass jar, or jars. The curd will keep in the refrigerator for up to 2 weeks.

7. Enjoy on buttered toast or biscuits. Spread on matza. Swirl through yogurt. You'll find many ways to use it.

CHAPTER FIVE

Sh'mini Atzeret

*The waning moon
turns her head
toward the returning rains,
essential to seed and nurture
next year's crops.*

From the Rabbi

Susan: *Why is the prayer for rain begun on the last day of Sukkot, instead of before? Don't you need rain to have a good harvest?*

Zoe: After the abundance of the seven-day festival of Sukkot, Zeman Simchateinu (The Time of Our Rejoicing), we are given the gift of an extra day, one added to the holiday yet independent in name and function. Torah directs us, "On the eighth day, you shall have a solemn assembly, you shall not work."[36] Sh'mini Atzeret (The Eighth Day of Assembly) offers us time to allow all that has come before to coalesce within us. The same way that food we have eaten transmutes into energy and nutrients for our body, we have an opportunity to do just that with everything we experienced during Sukkot. It's the day the Divine asks us to stay for but one more day.

Sufficient rain in its proper season was required for what hopefully was an abounding harvest. Now, we need to turn our attention to the next season with prayers for rain so that all the seeds we have sown, both inwardly and outwardly, may be properly nurtured throughout the coming months. Just as we are about to end and restart our cycle of public Torah reading on Simchat Torah, our cycle of beginning and ending and beginning again is mirrored here with our prayers for rain. Israel being the dry place it is, we can never take the rain for granted.

---

36 Numbers 29:35

The rain brings an affirmation of life's cyclical motion and it's the opportune time to amplify our thanksgiving.

Is Sh'mini Atzeret considered a festival?

One of the most fascinating aspects of this holiday takes a bit of sleuthing to uncover. I always marvel that Torah names three festivals, each celebrating a season: Pesach (spring), Shavuot (summer), and Sukkot (fall), but what about our fourth season, winter? Shavuot is Pesach's *atzeret* (the extra day), the fulfillment added to that festival. As we will see in the chapter on Shavuot, it needed Pesach to be fully realized. And having 49 days to process Pesach and prepare for Shavuot aids us immensely in being able to internalize the experience.

Pesach and Sukkot are exactly six months apart, both occurring on a full moon, holding our calendar in balance like hands of a scale. Where then is our winter festival and don't we need one? The answer can be found in the teachings by the Talmudic sage Rabbi Joshua ben Levi. He explains that Sukkot's atzeret—its added day—should have been, like Pesach's, 50 days after the festival.[37] However, as we see with other holidays, the way they were observed when the temple stood in Jerusalem, changed after its destruction. Some rituals could never be enacted without the temple, some morphed with the times, and some kept certain elements intact. In the case of Sh'mini Atzeret, the reason the sages decided it should be celebrated immediately after Sukkot was purely practical. Our ancestors made long, arduous pilgrimages to reach the temple, and then of course, after the festival, there was the trek home. It was too precarious for people to do this in the wintertime, which is the rainy season in Israel, due to unpredictable weather. Instead, the winter festival was set to immediately follow the fall festival, enabling our ancestors to contemplate the coming of winter, while getting back home long before that season began.

Is there something else I should know about Sh'mini Atzeret?

It is a magnificent tradition we have, that at the most joyous of occasions, just when we may be acutely aware of who is no longer with us, who is missing at our table, we set aside time to remember and pray for them. We offer Yizkor (Remember) memorial prayers on Yom Kippur, and on the three festivals; the last day of Pesach, on Shavuot, and on Sh'mini Atzeret, counted here as the last

---

37   Midrash Rabbah: Song of Songs 7:4

day of Sukkot. We say special prayers for the assent of the souls of those who have gone before us. And just as we sit with all the memories that well up within us, we can't help but be awed by the cycles within cycles of life.

By setting aside time like this and having a service in memory of our loved ones, we don't need to pretend that everything is whole or that everything is OK, because for some, it is not. Here we can acknowledge within our hearts, anything unresolved with someone who has passed. We can sit with painful memories, we can consider, we can pray and work

It is a magnificent tradition we have, that at the most joyous of occasions, just when we may be acutely aware of who is no longer with us, who is missing at our table, we set aside time to remember and pray for them.

toward a healing in our relationship that never happened during the lifetime of the person we are remembering. We also have the opportunity and wholehearted invitation to recall the love, yes, the love, the bond between us and our loved ones, the love that death can never take from us.

What is the essence of Sh'mini Atzeret?

On Sh'mini Atzeret, our time in the sukkah is winding down. We are truly turning our attention away from autumn and toward winter with our prayers for rain. Rabbi Yochanan taught that rain descends because of God's power, therefore, The Key of Rain is held in the Hands of the Holy One.[38] What a glorious image! I love picturing the Divine unlocking the heavens with a giant key, followed by rain falling from the clouds onto every plant, giving each one exactly what it needs. As we pray for our crops to receive this blessing, we pray, too, for ourselves. May we also receive all that we need to reach our greatest potential. May we remember The Holder of the Key, the One Who Gives Life, and give thanks.

38   Talmud, Ta'anit 2a–b

From the Cook

Zoe has explained that Sh'mini Atzeret is an added day of Sukkot—a gathering because the past days were so much fun. It's a time to bid farewell to autumn and get ready to hunker down for a new season. Winter may not always be cold where you live; however, the days will be shorter. Shorter, darker days bring on a desire for both substantial food and for something a bit lighter, as a reminder that as the last of the year's crops are harvested, there are already plans for the new ones coming up before you know it. Celebrate as you might with any other special day on the Jewish calendar with your favorite foods—beef brisket, roast chicken, knishes, babka—or give these recipes a try.

Finocchi alla Giudia

SERVES 4 TO 6

2 tablespoons olive oil

2 garlic cloves, peeled and slightly smashed

4 large fennel bulbs, fronds and outer tough leaves removed and discarded, quartered and rinsed

½ teaspoon salt

¾ cup water

½ cup Pastis or another anise-flavored liqueur

Optional garnish: 1 to 2 teaspoons dry-toasted fennel seeds

For centuries, fennel was considered a "Jew food." Perhaps because the beautiful pale green bulb, with its aniselike flavor and fragrance, was brought to Italy by Jewish traders who found it growing along the Mediterranean Sea shores of the countries of their North African business associates. I've upped the anise taste of this classic Jewish-style fennel recipe by adding Pastis to the cooking liquid and garnishing it with toasted fennel seeds. Search out wild Sicilian fennel seeds, if possible. They're small and packed with pure flavor.

1. Heat the olive oil in a deep, wide skillet over medium heat. When the oil is hot, add the garlic and sauté until very pale gold, 60 to 90 seconds.

2. Add the fennel and salt and toss to coat.

3. Add the water and Pastis. Cover, lower the heat to medium-low, and simmer until the fennel is fork-tender, 30 to 35 minutes. Remove from the heat and taste for seasoning.

4. Serve warm or at room temperature with the fennel seed garnish (if using).

Albondigas in Tomato-Tamarind Sauce

MAKES SIXTEEN 1½-INCH MEATBALLS

SAUCE

¼ cup olive oil

1 cup chopped yellow onion

2 garlic cloves, chopped

One 28-ounce can peeled tomatoes

1 teaspoon salt

¼ teaspoon Aleppo red pepper flakes

1 tablespoon tamarind paste thinned with 2 teaspoons of water (see Note)

1 tablespoon date syrup

1 teaspoon grated fresh ginger

1 teaspoon ground cumin

1 teaspoon ground cinnamon

ALBONDIGAS

1 pound ground beef

¼ cup finely chopped yellow onion

1 large egg, beaten

¼ cup panko bread crumbs

¼ cup chopped fresh flat-leaf parsley

½ teaspoon salt

¼ teaspoon freshly ground black pepper, or to taste

¼ cup all-purpose flour for dredging

⅓ cup neutral oil, such as canola, for frying

Serving options: Mamaliga (page 72), rice

You may be familiar with *albondigas* as the main ingredient in a Mexican meatball soup. However, the provenance of those little meatballs stretches far back to the 15th century, when the word was derived from the Arabic *al-bunduq*, which means "hazelnut," a reference to their size. The Ladino-speaking Sephardic Jews called them by their Spanish-dialect name, *albondigas*. The meatballs are popular in Israel, where the Diaspora population adds ingredients from their native cuisines to personalize them. That's what I've done. Don't be alarmed by the long list of ingredients—it's an easy-to-put-together recipe.

MAKE THE SAUCE

1. Heat the olive oil in a saucepan or deep skillet over medium-high heat. Add the onion and garlic. Cook, stirring, until the onion is translucent, about 2 minutes. Squeeze the tomatoes through your hands into the oil. Add the salt, Aleppo pepper flakes, tamarind paste, date syrup, ginger, cumin, and cinnamon. Lower the heat to medium-low and simmer the sauce while you make the albondigas.

MAKE THE ALBONDIGAS

1. Place the ground beef in a bowl. Add the onion, egg, panko, salt, black pepper, and parsley. Use your hands to thoroughly combine the ingredients.

2. Spread the flour on a dinner plate or small tray.

3. Wet your hands to help you easily form 2-inch albondigas (they will shrink to about 1½ inches when cooked). Roll them in the flour.

4. Heat the neutral oil in a medium skillet over medium-high heat. Fry the floured albondigas in batches, turning them so all sides brown. Transfer the browned albondigas directly into the simmering tomato sauce.

5. Simmer until the albondigas are cooked through and they and the sauce have taken on each other's flavors, about 30 minutes.

6. Serve hot.

NOTE: *You may find containers of tamarind labeled "paste," but some are really more like a very thick syrup—the latter is preferable. If you use paste, use a bit less to allow for some water to thin it to a syrup.*

Cranberry-Apple Cobbler
with Plant-Based Milk Pouring Custard

SERVES 6 TO 8

FRUIT

2 tablespoons unsalted
  butter, plus more for
  baking dish

1 orange

1 cup sugar

1 cup cranberries, rinsed and
  picked through

4 large Mutsu or Granny
  Smith apples, peeled,
  cored, and cut into
  1½-inch chunks

½ teaspoon ground cinnamon

Pinch of ground allspice

BISCUITS

2 cups all-purpose flour, plus
  more for dusting

2 tablespoons sugar

1 tablespoon baking powder

½ teaspoon baking soda

Pinch of salt

6 tablespoons (¾ stick)
  unsalted butter, cut into
  bits and chilled

1 cup buttermilk, plus more
  for glazing

Melted butter for brushing

½ cup slivered almonds

As Sh'Mini Atzeret ushers in the dark of a new season, celebrate with this bright cobbler made with the wealth of fruit—cranberries, apples, and oranges—that Mother Nature has provided to guide us through less-light days.

1. Make the fruit: Heat the oven to 350°F. Lightly butter a low-sided 2-quart baking dish.

2. Use a vegetable peeler to remove half of the zest from the orange and place in a food processor. Juice the unzested orange half and set aside. (Save the rest of the zested orange for another use.) Add the sugar to the zest and process until the zest is finely minced and the sugar is orange colored. Transfer to a medium bowl. Put the cranberries in the food processor and pulse until coarsely chopped. Transfer to the bowl of sugar. Add the apples, orange juice, cinnamon, and allspice. Toss well and place in the prepared baking dish. Dot with the 2 tablespoons of butter.

3. Make the biscuits: Combine the flour, sugar, baking powder, baking soda, and salt in a large bowl. Cut the chilled butter into the flour mixture with a pastry blender or two dinner knives until the mixture resembles coarse cornmeal. Add the buttermilk and toss with a fork until the dough starts to come together.

4. Turn out the dough onto a floured work surface and knead lightly and quickly until smooth. Pat the dough with floured hands to about ½ inch thick. Use a 2-inch-diameter biscuit cutter to cut out rounds. Gently press the scraps together, knead again, and cut more biscuits—

you will probably need all the dough to cover the fruit. Brush the biscuits with melted butter and scatter the almonds over the top.

5. Bake the cobbler until the biscuits are nicely browned and the fruit is bubbling, about 45 minutes. Remove from the oven and let cool on a rack.

6. Serve warm or at room temperature with a splash of Plant-Based Milk Pouring Custard (page 26).

CHAPTER SIX

Simchat Torah

In her wisdom,
the moon wanes,
while we dance the cycles
of completion and renewal.

From the Rabbi

Susan: *What makes Simchat Torah a raucous, overwhelmingly joyous holiday?*

Zoe: Sometimes people think that the High Holy Days end with Yom Kippur or maybe even extend through Sukkot (The Season of Our Rejoicing). However, after a week of celebrations in the sukkah, and giving thanks for all we have received from every direction in our lives, our joy is extended and increased with an added day, the celebration of Sh'mini Atzeret (The Eighth Day of Assembly). As remarkable as this is, it doesn't end here. We are gifted with yet another sacred holiday, Simchat Torah (literally, Rejoicing with the Torah). There is nothing quite like this holy day when all the momentum that has been gathering, all the seeds that have been sown, and all the prayers that have been said reach their climax with a release of irrepressible joy.

As Torah lives at the core of our teachings, Simchat Torah feels as though it is Misinai—something handed down directly from Mount Sinai. But it wasn't until the 10th century that this holiday came into being. Prior to this, there were two customs for the reading of Torah—the Five Books of Moses: Genesis, Exodus, Leviticus, Numbers, and Deuteronomy—in the Babylonian tradition the Torah was read over the course of one year, while the Palestinian tradition was a triennial cycle. If there was to be a celebration of the fulfillment of that cycle, it could have only taken place every three years. After coexisting for 1,000 years, the influence of the Babylonian custom spread. With inspiration, our sages chose to unify the practice of Torah reading within an annual cycle, enabling a yearly rejoicing in its completion. If there was ever a reason to create a new holiday, this was it. Of course, it had to be determined where in our calendar this would take place. Up until then, Sh'mini Atzeret had been a two-day holiday and it was concluded that, going forward, its second day would be given over to this new holiday, Simchat Torah.

In Israel, Sh'mini Atzeret and Simchat Torah are observed on the same day, the 22nd of the Hebrew month of Tishrei. In the Diaspora, the Reform movement adheres to this as well. However, the rest of the Jewish world celebrates Sh'mini Atzeret on the 22nd and Simchat Torah on the 23rd of Tishrei.

A stirring aspect of this holiday happens in both the evening and morning services in synagogue when the Torahs are taken from the ark, lovingly embraced, and danced with in seven *hakafot* (circuits) around the sanctuary. In some communities, the dancing even extends out into the streets. It is a procession reminiscent of the seventh day of Sukkot, Hoshana Rabbah (the great Hoshann). While holding our lulav and etrog, we make seven hakafot around the Torah while praying, "Please, bring us salvation." Both of these rituals echo the seven circles made by one beloved around the other in a Jewish wedding ceremony. Seven, the sacred number of completion, the day of Shabbat, the one given to us by the Divine, appears and reappears in myriad ways in our tradition and always with joy.

Each *hakafa* has its own theme. For many years, on the eve of Simchat Torah, we have been blessed to have Klezmer Berl's Hotsie Totsie Posse, a multipiece klezmer band, play different melodies for each hakafa, helping to take us higher and higher after we pray each refrain, "Adonai, please save us, Adonai, please grant us success, Adonai, please answer us on the day we call."

The liturgy of these seven hakafot is one of my favorites because of the poignant, focused, powerful pleas and for the variety of names reflecting different aspects of the Divine: God of Spirits, Speaker of Righteousness, Pure and Right, the One Who Knows, Eternal Sovereign, Helper of the Poor, and Holy and Awesome. The Torahs are passed from one to another so that everyone can have the opportunity to be close to and dance with the Torah. We have small replica and plush Torahs for the children, who delight in being able to move freely around amid so much motion, music, and joy.

During the evening service, many communities, including ours, enact a unique and dramatic ritual where we can see the miracle of Torah unfold. All our attention turns to one Torah while the remaining ones are respectfully returned to the ark. Everyone forms a huge circle around the room as the band begins a new *niggun* (a song without words). Her white velvet *mantel* (the covering embroidered with lush golden threads) is removed. Her *gartel* (velvet sash) is unbuckled, and she is gently and carefully opened literally and figuratively, held up by the hands of every adult in attendance, revealing each letter, forming each word, filling each book in all her glory.

With the Torah open, we can literally see all five Books—Genesis, Exodus, Leviticus, Numbers, and Deuteronomy—that were eloquently handwritten in Hebrew by a *sofer* (scribe). Witnessing the entire Torah revealed and seeing the end of Devarim (Deuteronomy) meet up with the beginning of Bereshit (Genesis) is quite awe-inducing. There is really nothing quite like this moment. Once everyone has had a chance to be with the Torah and before arms begin to tire, a new melody is sounded and the strenuous task of rolling the scroll back is completed. The Torah is then lovingly carried to the Torah table. We have seen the Torah; now it is time to hear it.

Before each Torah reading, an *aliyah* (literally, ascending), which is a special honor, is given to a person or people. Normally someone is first called to the Torah when they become bar or bat mitzvah, but on Simchat Torah, when our joy cannot be contained, all the children are invited up for the aliyah of the penultimate reading of Deuteronomy. Often a large tallit (prayer shawl) or many are held up over their heads as the adults call out blessings for them. The Chatan Torah (the Groom of the Torah) or Kallat Torah (the Bride of the Torah) is called up for the honor of the last reading of Deuteronomy. The final honor is given to Chatan Bereshit or Kallat Bereshit (the Groom or Bride of Genesis) before we immediately restart our Torah cycle by reading the beginning of Genesis. We follow the custom in our synagogue that many do, of including everyone in these last two honors so that we all can be under the holy wings of Torah.

This scroll containing the esoteric code, the blueprint of our lives, holds the faith, hope, and dreams of our people. It also may contain stories that make us uncomfortable, things we don't know what to make of, and things no one seems to understand. Still, this is our Torah. We are taught, "Turn it and turn it again, for all is in it; see through it, grow old and worn in it, do not budge from it, for there is nothing that works better than it."[39] In this famous quote from Mishnah, Rabbi Ben Bag-Bag directs us to keep returning to Torah even when we don't understand it. Keep looking at it, he urges, from every possible angle. Our sages whose teachings we read in the Mishnah, Talmud, and other sacred writings, share varying and often opposing views of what the Torah is saying.

39 Mishnah: Pirkei Avot 5:22

And yet, all these opinions are valued and recorded. Whether we understand a word of Mishnah or not, I imagine we have all experienced the value and have benefitted from looking at something from a new angle. This insight encourages us to be patient with ourselves as we turn and return to the study of Torah.

I heard that there's a tradition of drinking and throwing candy into the crowd of revelers to celebrate the idea that Torah is sweet. Do you do these things in your synagogue?

As for the sweets, Judaism has a long history of connecting them to Torah. When children learn their *alef-bet* (alphabet), they are given something sweet to connect sweetness with Torah. After Torah is read in synagogue, candies are often tossed in the air, again reminding us of the sweetness of Torah. In my community, on Simchat Torah, we give little gift bags of candy to people as they leave. This cuts down on the possible danger of someone slipping on a piece of candy during the dancing and leaves the sugar rush, and subsequent crash, in the hands of the parents and out of ours.

Every synagogue is different, and the customs really do vary. As alcohol is connected to the idea of increasing our joy, in some synagogues you will find people making a L'Chayim (To Life), a toast—or many, for that matter. On the other extreme, there are also synagogues, concerned about the overuse of alcohol, which have replaced it totally with grape juice.

As we all take our leave of the sanctuary, I pray not to take leave of our Torah. I pray for us all, that our legs transform to become hers, that every step leads us to do one more mitzvah, that the pinnacle of joy that has snowballed in this moment propels us forward so that we may spread the joy we have tasted with everyone we meet.

> The ritual of fully opening the Torah on Simchat Torah was started by Rabbi Zalman Schachter-Shalomi of blessed memory. I had the honor of learning it from Rabbi Jonathan Kligler, at Kehillat Lev Shalem, the Woodstock Jewish Congregation in Woodstock, New York. The minhag (custom) was to have several Torah readers walk around the room and translate the Torah that was in front of each person, giving each the opportunity to contemplate that passage for the entire year.

From the Cook

Reading what Zoe has written about the sheer joyousness of Simchat Torah has inspired me to share some of my seasonal recipes that fit right in with this holiday. Just as with all holiday dishes, I take my cue from the availability of ingredients.

If you're in Egypt for a Simchat Torah celebration, you might find a table filled with meze, an offering of small appetizer dishes, such as hummus, *ful medammas* (fava bean spread), baba ghanoush, assorted olives, dried fruits and nuts, and so on, served with piles of warm, fluffy pita bread.

There's symbolism attached to the tradition of making rolled foods during Simchat Torah as they resemble the Torah.

Rainbow Chard Rolls

MAKES 8 ROLLS; SERVES 4 AS A SIDE DISH

8 large chard leaves, long stems included

1 cup uncooked basmati rice

2 tablespoons olive oil

2 large garlic cloves, chopped finely

2 heaping tablespoons chopped raisins

2 heaping tablespoons chopped almonds

¼ cup chopped fresh chives

Additional chopped herbs (optional)

¼ teaspoon Aleppo pepper flakes, or more to taste

Salt

I like to think that chard, with its bright rainbow-colored ribs, is a continuing gift from my sister of blessed memory, Laura. I always found a hedge of them growing in her spectacular Nantucket garden when I arrived on the island for my annual August visit. Since she passed away, my brother-in-law has kept up her tradition of planting it, and there continues to be rainbow chard to greet my visits. One summer, I made this dish. I've wanted to make stuffed chard leaves for a while. Stuffed vegetables reach their apex in Middle Eastern, North African, and eastern Mediterranean countries' cuisine. I'm especially interested in the stuffed vegetable preparations that are created in Israel, where they're called *memulaim* (stuffed ones). Israel, home to immigrants from all over the Jewish Diaspora, have added their culinary ways to what has become the cuisine of Israel.

1. Line a surface with a double layer of paper towels. Bring a large pot of water to a boil and blanch the chard leaves for 30 seconds. Use tongs to transfer them to the paper towels to drain. Straighten out the leaves. Reserve ½ cup of the blanching liquid.

2. Cut off each stem, starting with the widest part inside the leaf (the rib), creating a V at the base. Set aside the leaves and cut the stems into small dice.

3. Cook the rice in copious amounts of fresh water until tender. Drain and set aside.

4. Heat 1 tablespoon of the olive oil in a medium skillet over medium heat. Add the garlic and cook until pale gold. Add the chopped chard stems and stir in with the garlic, then add the raisins and almonds. Cook until the almonds are golden and appear crunchy, a minute or two.

5. Heat the oven to 375°F. Use 1½ teaspoons of the remaining olive oil to coat a baking dish that can accommodate eight stuffed rolls. Add the ½ cup of the reserved blanching liquid.

6. Transfer the rice to a bowl. Add the chard stem mixture to the rice. Add the chives (and other herbs, if desired). Toss together to thoroughly combine.

7. Place 2 heaping tablespoons of the rice mixture on each chard leaf. Tuck the sides over the mixture and roll up the leaf so it resembles a cigar. Place the chard rolls in the prepared baking dish. Drizzle the remaining 1½ teaspoons of olive oil over the top. Cover with parchment paper or foil and bake until the chard rolls are hot and the leaves are tender. They should retain their color.

8. Serve hot, warm, or at room temperature.

Carciofi Fritti

BATTER-FRIED ARTICHOKES

SERVES 4

1 large lemon

6 medium artichokes

1 cup all-purpose flour

1 teaspoon salt

1 cup icy-cold seltzer

1 cup neutral oil, such as
canola, or more as needed

Optional garnishes: lemon
wedges, flaky sea salt

Of all the wonderful artichoke recipes that are included in the lexicon of Jewish recipes—and there are many—I gravitate to this one. For me, this style is sentimental because I tasted artichokes prepared this way during my first trip to Italy. When I bravely bit in to its piping hot, crisp exterior only to be met with something that I would describe as artichoke cream, I nearly cried with joy. *Ancora,* more.

I made sure to call the recipe "batter"-fried artichokes so they wouldn't be mistaken for the most famous of all Italian artichoke recipes, *carciofi alla giudia,* sometimes referred to as simply fried artichokes. My friend Olga Cipolla walked me through this recipe and taught me the importance of using seltzer in the batter. The gassy bubbles in the seltzer allow the batter to rise to a light and crisply fluffy texture—not unlike tempura.

1. Prepare the artichokes: Cut the lemon in half and squeeze both halves into a large bowl of water. Working with one artichoke at a time, cut off the exposed (black) part of the stem and peel the remainder. Remove the outside leaves by bending them backward and pulling down; they'll snap at the "meaty" point of the leaf. Pull away leaves until you see only pale green ones, at about the halfway point of the artichoke. Use a very sharp knife to cut away the remaining leaves. Quarter the artichoke. Cut out the fuzzy choke. Use a very sharp knife to cut each quarter in half or into thirds. Immediately add the pieces to the lemon water to prevent them from turning brown. Repeat the process with the remaining artichokes.

2. Make the *pastella* (batter). Combine the flour and salt in a large bowl. Whisk in the seltzer, carefully breaking up lumps.

3. Remove the artichokes from the water and pat dry with paper towels. Immerse them in the batter, taking care that they thoroughly absorb it.

4. Place a large, deep skillet over medium-high heat. Add the oil. When the oil bubbles around a wooden chopstick inserted into it, it's ready. Fry the artichokes in batches. Use the chopstick to flip them around the oil until they are golden on all sides, about 5 minutes. Use tongs to transfer them to a paper towel–lined plate to drain.

5. Serve hot with a squeeze of lemon and flaky sea salt, if desired.

Artichokes became a popular ingredient in Italian Jewish food when the Saracens brought them to the shores of Sicily and the local Jewish population immediately used them in their kitchens. As Sicilian Jews moved north through the mainland peninsula, they brought their now loved artichokes with them. As they journeyed north, artichoke recipes developed into the popular fried artichoke, the calling card of Roman ghetto; the batter-fried artichokes of Tuscany; and the first dish I learned to make when I lived in Milan, *risotto ai carciofi* (risotto with artichokes).

Socca with Radicchio and Fennel Salad

Socca is a chickpea flour pancake. You'll find various iterations of the preparation in coastal Mediterranean spots from Marseille to Messina, where they're called *panisse, farinata,* and *panelle.* The cooked pancake, cut into wedges, can be simply served instead of bread with a bowl of soup, or as its own course, like this one topped with vegetables roasted or raw.

SERVES 6

SALAD DRESSING

1 teaspoon Dijon mustard

1 teaspoon finely chopped fresh rosemary

2 teaspoons apple cider vinegar

½ teaspoon salt

A few grinds of black pepper

¼ cup olive oil

SOCCA

1 cup chickpea flour

½ teaspoon salt

1 tablespoon finely chopped fresh rosemary

2 tablespoons extra-virgin olive oil

1 cup warm water

TO ASSEMBLE

2 cups thinly sliced fennel (1 large bulb)

2 cups thinly sliced radicchio

MAKE THE SALAD DRESSING

1. Combine the mustard, rosemary, vinegar, salt, and pepper in a small bowl. Whisk in the olive oil until a tight emulsion is achieved. Set aside.

MAKE THE SOCCA

1. Heat the oven to 450°F. Place a 10-inch cast-iron skillet in the oven.

2. Combine the chickpea flour, salt, rosemary and 1 tablespoon of the olive oil in a separate bowl. Whisk in the warm water to create a smooth batter.

3. Drench the tip of a rolled-up paper towel in the remaining tablespoon of olive oil. Use it to oil the hot cast-iron skillet. Pour the chickpea batter into the pan. Shake the pan to ensure that the batter spreads evenly over the entire bottom. Bake until set and golden, about 15 minutes. Remove from the oven and let cool for 5 minutes.

ASSEMBLE THE SOCCA

1. Combine the fennel and radicchio in a large bowl. Add the dressing and toss to thoroughly coat the vegetables.

2. To serve, cut the socca into six wedges. Place each serving on a plate and pile the salad on top. Serve immediately.

Bacalao a la Vizcaina

SERVES 4

1 pound salt cod

½ cup olive oil

2 cups coarsely chopped yellow onions (about 2 medium onions)

3 garlic cloves chopped

Pinch of hot red pepper flakes (optional)

1 pound small potatoes, quartered

One 28-ounce can peeled tomatoes, crushed with your hands

1 cup dry white wine

1 teaspoon ground cumin

1 teaspoon smoked paprika

1 bay leaf

1 tablespoon capers

½ cup small, pimiento-stuffed green olives

½ cup coarsely chopped fresh flat-leaf parsley

Salt, if needed, to taste

The Crypto (hidden) Jews of Spain and Portugal lived religious lives inside their home while declaring another religious faith outside their home, for fear of expulsion from their home country or forced conversion to Catholicism. Like all the Jews of the Diaspora, wherever they lived in the world, they adapted the cuisine of their home country to kosher dietary law. This salt cod dish, which originated in the Basque area of Spain, was a particular favorite. It's an easy one to bring into the kosher kitchen as none of the ingredients are *treif* (unfit to Jewish law).

Salt cod has a long shelf life. Make this recipe with all long-shelf-life ingredients to create a dish worthy of celebration. I like to serve this with Mamaliga (page 72).

1. Soak the salt cod for at least 4 hours, changing the water two or three times for up to 24 hours. Rinse after the final soak.

2. Place the soaked and rinsed cod in a large pot of water over medium-high heat. Bring a boil. Lower the heat to a simmer and cook for 15 to 20 minutes, until the fish is fork-tender.

3. Drain the fish and use a fork to flake it into small pieces. Set aside.

4. Heat the olive oil in a large skillet over medium heat. When the oil is hot, add the onions, garlic, and hot pepper flakes. Sauté until the onions are translucent. Add the potatoes, tomatoes, wine, cumin, smoked paprika, and bay leaf. Lower the heat to a simmer and cook until the potatoes are tender, about 15 minutes.

5. Add the fish, capers, and olives. Toss together and heat for 5 minutes.

6. Toss in the parsley. Taste for salt. The cod is still salty, as are the capers and olives.

7. Serve immediately.

101

Tahini and Dried Fruit Balls

**MAKES TWELVE TO
FOURTEEN 1½-INCH BALLS**

14 large Medjool dates, pitted

½ cup walnuts

¼ cup tahini

1 tablespoon good-quality
unsweetened cocoa
powder (I use Valrhona
brand)

¼ teaspoon salt

Dried, unsweetened coconut
flakes

In Memory's Kitchen is a poignant book that the late, great author Cara De Silva put together with recipes gathered from the women of the Czechoslovakian concentration camp Terezín. The famished women wrote recipes on scraps of purloined paper to help allay their hunger and establish hope for a return home. The recipes are rich with memories of such ingredients as dried fruits, nuts, butter, and cream. The collection inspired me to develop this dried fruit confection. Consider wrapping individual tahini balls in cellophane, then showering them on the dinner table at the end of a celebratory meal, or adding them to Purim (page 138) gift bags, or *shalach manos* or *mishloach manot* (gift baskets).

1. Combine the dates, walnuts, tahini, cocoa powder, and salt in a food processor. Run the machine until the mixture becomes a thick paste.

2. Spread the coconut flakes on a dinner plate or small tray.

3. Form 1-inch balls of the date paste. Roll them around in the coconut to coat completely. They can be refrigerated, covered, for up to a few weeks.

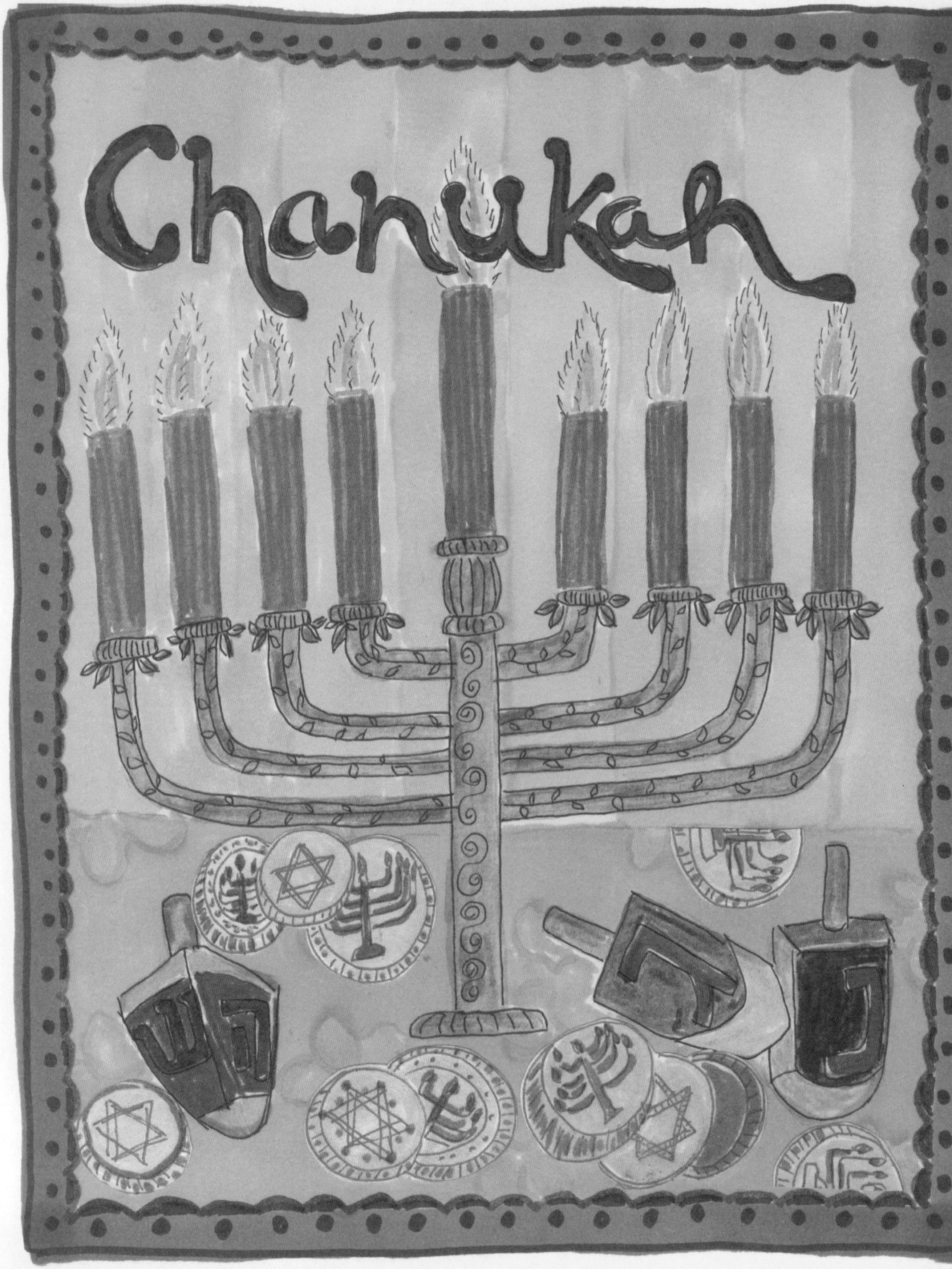
Chanukah

CHAPTER SEVEN

Chanukah

She disappears
and we wait
for what Adam and Eve couldn't know,
that she always returns
with the warmth of the sun's reflection
on her face.

From the Rabbi

Susan: *Chanukah is known for its candle lighting, dreidel playing, and, eating fried foods. What's the inspiration behind these holiday rituals?*
Zoe: The story of Chanukah, although not biblically commanded, echoes back to a core biblical mitzvah given a thousand years earlier. From the time the Aseret HaDebrot (The Ten Sayings), otherwise known as the Ten Commandments, were given on Mount Sinai, and after the massive turning away from the Divine culminating in the creation of the golden calf, the Holy One instructed the Israelites to build the Mishkan (Tabernacle), the portable, mystical, and holy sanctuary. This directive was an expression of God's forgiveness for the people's transgression and the reestablished covenant with them. Hashem said, "And they shall make a holy place, and I will dwell among them."[40] And so it was that inside the Mishkan, the Holy Presence lived.

You may wonder, what this has to do with Chanukah, and the answer is, "Everything." The Mishkan, completed on the 25th of Kislev, was where the Divine instructed Moses that his brother Aaron would light and keep the lamps burning in front of the curtain protecting the ark and its sacred contents.[41] This was continued for all the years our ancestors journeyed in the desert. When they finally crossed into the Promised Land, the Mishkan continued to be used

---

40   Exodus 25:8
41   Leviticus 24:1–4

for almost 500 years until the Beit HaMikdash (Holy Temple) in Jerusalem—the new, magnificent dwelling place for the Divine—was built by King Solomon. Contained within was a seven-branched menorah that was lit daily. When the (First) Temple was destroyed and rebuilt, a seven-branched menorah was once again aflame in the Second Temple. It was during this time that the *beit kenesset* (place of gathering, or synagogue) came into existence. Today, when we enter a synagogue anywhere in the world, we will likely see a seven-branched menorah somewhere in the sanctuary and a *ner tamid* (eternal light) suspended above the *aron kodesh* (holy ark), carrying on the mitzvah enacted in the desert and in both temples. When we light our Chanukiah (Chanukah menorah), we are continuing the same tradition begun by Aaron over 3,000 years ago. Now that's a *dayenu* moment.

The eight-day holiday of Chanukah begins on the 25th of Kislev. For those of us living in the Northern Hemisphere, our days have gradually been getting shorter while the nights have lengthened. It is a cold time of year and by the 25th of this lunar month, we are fast approaching the winter solstice where we will experience the shortest and darkest day of our year. Rabbi Jill Hammer describes, "The new moon is a symbol of eternal renewal, and the full moon is focused on the present. The last weeks of the months are focused on the hopes and fears for the future."[42] This is a time when we overwhelm the darkness and any accompanying fears by lighting the lights of Chanukah.

Our story takes place over 2,000 years ago, when the Syrian-Greek Empire ruled Israel. Under the rule of King Antiochus IV Epiphanes, it became illegal for the Jews to live openly and carry out their time-honored rituals. A three-year war ensued between the well-established, trained army and a band of locals led by Mattathias and his son Judas Maccabeus. During this time, the Greeks captured and defiled the Holy Temple, offering pig sacrifices upon the altar. Miraculously, the untrained group of men were able to outwit the soldiers, recapture their temple, and become victors in battle. As the temple was being repaired, only one cruse of oil was found, just enough to light the temple menorah for a day. What a boon to the recovery and healing process that this oil mysteriously burned instead for eight days, just the time it took to prepare new olive oil for the lamps. On the 25th of Kislev, a new altar was installed, and the temple was rededicated. Chanukah was born. It was determined that every year, a nine-branched menorah would be lit for each of the eight days the miracle lasted, plus one *shamash* (helper) candle to ignite the others. As we light our Chanukah (rededication) menorah, we thank the Holy One as we recall our ancestors who stood up against oppression and victoriously gained their hard-won religious and personal freedom.

42 Tel Shemesh, Jewish Cycles of the Moon, by Rabbi Jill Hammer (temshemesh.org).

I know that one candle is lit on the first night of Chanukah and then increased by one on each of the following nights. However, I heard you say that, one year, you lit all the candles on the first night and then decreased them by one each following night. Why?

I was conducting an experiment. You see, in the Talmud, there is a wonderful discourse between two famous scholars and their schools, Beit Shammai (The House of Shammai) and Beit Hillel (The House of Hillel). It was Beit Shammai that taught that we should light eight candles the first night, seven on the next, and so forth, so that on the last night, we would light only one. On the other hand, Beit Hillel taught us to light one candle the first night, two the second, and so on, until the last night, when we would light all eight.[43] We know Beit Hillel won that dispute as was almost always the case when they disagreed, as it is the ritual we follow. However, I always found this particular debate fascinating and wondered what it might be like to try Beit Shammai's way. It seemed to me that, living in New York as I do, lighting one additional candle each night makes perfect sense because as the days are short and the nights long, I am increasing the light. But I often think about our friends in the Southern Hemisphere whose days are wildly long and bright during Chanukah evenings and I thought that if I lived in Australia, for example, following Beit Shammai's teaching might make perfect sense. So, even though I had not left New York, I thought I would try the other approach. For me, it was an energizing experiment as I appreciated just having a different experience for that one year. I did return to Beit Hillel's directive, however, with increased *kavanah* (intention).

Because Chanukah often comes at the same time of year as Christmas, they often get caught up in the same kind of holiday commercialism. What would you say to distinguish the celebrations?

We can see that this is a very distinctive holiday. It is only connected to Christmas by proximity of date. However, many of us really get into the mode of buying a lot of presents. In this way, some people feel it has competed with Christmas, but truly both holidays are uniquely their own. Although not qualified to teach about Christmas, I can say with confidence that neither Christmas nor Chanukah is about what or how many gifts we give or receive, not that I'm trying to debunk the joyful art of giving. Ask my daughter and you will discover that I err on the side of abundant gifting.

We know that candle lighting is a treasured mitzvah within Judaism. We light candles at home or in synagogue before the onset of Shabbat and the festivals as well as when they are concluded, not only marking their completion

43   Talmud, Shabbat 21b

but specifically distinguishing those festive times from the rest of the week. Unlike these indoor rituals, Chanukah candle lighting was originally done just outside the left entrance of the home, just opposite the mezuzah. The idea was to advertise the miracle, share the good news, so to speak. Over time, in some locations because of fear of persecution, it became unsafe to publicize the lighting and the mitzvah was brought indoors, the menorah often being placed in the window. Now, many of us have it as the centerpiece of our Chanukah table.

You ask, What can be done to spread more teachings about this holiday? No one has done more than what Chabad Lubavitch has accomplished and continues to do to make Chanukah and every other holiday more visible throughout the world. In 1974, Rabbi Levi Shemtov and a few of his students created a 5-foot-tall Chanukah menorah that they lit in front of Independence Hall in Philadelphia. The following year, Rabbi Chaim Drizin lit one that was 22 feet tall in San Francisco. The *Rebbe*'s words of encouragement were like an accelerant. What started out as one candle lighting turned into several thousand Chabad-sponsored lightings taking place annually around the world. This has inspired others to create public candle-lighting celebrations in their own communities and beyond. One could easily think that this whole notion of placing the menorah outdoors was some modern concoction, but since we know this is what was originally done to celebrate the miracle, isn't it a brilliant combination of returning to our roots and expanding on them all at once?

In 1990, the Rebbe said, "God gave each of us a soul, which is a candle that He gives us to illuminate our surroundings with His light. We must not only illuminate the inside of our homes, but also the outside, and the world at large.... Go out into the courtyard into the public domain, and create light which illuminates the entire outside world."[44]

At our synagogue, we invite everyone to bring their own menorah; we provide the candles and extra menorahs if people don't have their own. It is stunning to see the variety of designs, materials, colors, and sizes as well as the stories that accompany the menorahs. Each year, our Hebrew school students make or decorate their own, so the tables are thankfully surrounded by people of every age. Our group candle lighting is especially amazing when done on the last night, where the room is literally filled with hundreds of candles. The sound of everyone singing the blessings, the glow of the many candles, and the feeling in the sanctuary provides a lot of spiritual fuel for us individually and communally.

The more we enact the candle-lighting ritual in our homes, teaching our children and sharing with loved ones, the more deeply we root these traditions within ourselves. Imagine being one of those little Chanukah candles, lit by

44   *Rebbe* by Joseph Telushkin, pp. 269–70

another, just out in the world spreading light everywhere we go. This is the tall order of the mitzvah of Chanukah.

I was thrilled to make a new discovery while writing this chapter. We know that Aaron was the menorah lighter in the Mishkan. He was also famous for having been a lover of peace, as we read in Mishnah, "Be amongst the disciples of Aaron, loving peace, pursuing peace, loving ordinary folk and bringing them near Torah."[45] The Sfat Emet,[46] explained Aaron, believed that every person, within their heart, longs to make reconciliation and peace.[47]

I now realize that Chanukah is a time for peace making! In Israel, there is even a tradition of feuding families to join together for meals during the holiday, and for anyone needing to heal a relationship, to come together for this purpose. "Hanukkah is an auspicious time to come closer to one another and for reconciliation. It is the great holiday of peace."[48] May the illumination born of peace making, find its way into all our hearts. *Chanukah Sameach* (Happy Chanukah), my friends.

---

45 Mishnah, Pirkei Avot 1:12
46 Rabbi Yehudah Aryeh Leib Alter of Gur, who went by the name of his book, *The Sfat Emet*
47 *The Light That Unites* by Aaron Goldsheider, Halpern Press
48 Ibid.

Asarah B'Tevet (The 10th of Tevet)

Our sages instituted four fast days during the year where we mark and mourn the destruction of the Beit HaMikdash (Holy Temple), both the First and Second Temples. The 10th of the Hebrew month of Tevet occurs in the month following Chanukah and just two weeks after its completion. The celebration and feasting on one, and a fasting and praying on the other, may seem like worlds apart, but both recall a time when our people were persecuted and murdered for their beliefs and way of life.

On this day in 425 BCE, King Nebuchadnezzar's Babylonian troops lay siege upon Jerusalem. After brutal battling for the next year and a half, the temple was destroyed.

Our sages teach, "It is a mitzvah, for every Jewish community, even when they are beset with trouble, God forbid, to fast and pray to Hashem, blessed be His Name, to be rescued from their troubles."[49] Today, as on all fast days, we say Selichot prayers, speaking in the singular and in the plural, reminding ourselves that we are responsible for our actions and for one another and for making this world a better place. We pray to forgive and to be forgiven. "Out of the depths I call to You. Oh Lord, hear my cry."[50]

---

49 Kitzer Shukchan Aruch, Laws Concerning Fast Days 121:11
50 Psalm 130:1

From the Cook

In 2014, the last night of Chanukah fell on Christmas Eve. I was on Nantucket to visit and celebrate the holidays with my sister Laura, of blessed memory, and her husband, Jim. Christmas celebrations were usually assigned to Jim as he was the gentile in the group and made us his family's traditional Christmas morning meal of crêpes and freshly squeezed orange juice. That year was different. I think, for some reason, Laura sensed her imminent passing, and reached back to our ancestors and made a Chanukah dinner for us—in her own unique style. She was a passionate gardener, so she made a menorah for the table by placing candles in a terra-cotta flowerpot, and the shamash (the candle that lights all the others) in a mini terra-cotta pot set into the larger pot. It was an intimate, dark, quiet, candle-lit Nantucket evening with the dim glow of the kitchen coming through to the dining room to help illuminate our table.

Fried food on Chanukah is a reminder of a miracle that helped the Hebrews restore their temple destroyed by invading Syrians. They found enough oil to fuel the temple lamps for one night. Instead, the lamps burned for eight nights. Cheese latkes, considered the original latke, is an Italian dish; Syrian Jews make pureed pumpkin fritters; in Morocco, *seffah*—sweet couscous flavored with cinnamon, sugar, and butter—is served; and *keftes de Prasa*, Sephardic leek fritters, is another fried food to add to the menu.

Mixed Vegetable Latkes

My sister Laura added parsnips and carrots, freshly pulled from her garden, plus storage potatoes, to make these colorful and herbaceous latkes.

MAKES ABOUT THIRTY 2-INCH PANCAKES; SERVES 6 TO 8

1½ pounds mature potatoes, peeled

½ pound parsnips, peeled

½ pound carrots, peeled

1 medium red onion, chopped finely

½ cup chopped fresh dill

3 tablespoons matza meal or unseasoned bread crumbs

1 teaspoon salt

½ teaspoon freshly ground white pepper

2 or 3 large eggs

Vegetable oil for frying

Optional garnishes: Eden's Applesauce (page 44), sour cream

1. Place a large fine-mesh sieve over a large bowl. Grate the potatoes and place in the sieve. Grate the parsnips and the carrots and place in a separate large bowl. Add the onion, dill, matza meal, salt, and white pepper to the parsnip mixture.

2. Using your hands, squeeze the potatoes, a palmful at a time, over the sieve to remove as much moisture as possible. Add the squeezed potatoes to the parsnip mixture. When all the potatoes have been squeezed, remove the sieve, and carefully pour off and discard the potato liquid, leaving the white potato starch at the bottom. Add the starch to the vegetable mixture. Add two of the eggs and thoroughly combine. Put a scant ¼ cup of the mixture into the palm of your hand. If the mixture sticks together, you can form the remaining mixture into cakes. If not, add another egg and then form the cakes.

3. Heat ½ inch of oil in a medium, heavy-bottomed skillet over medium heat. Place a few cakes in the hot oil and fry until dark gold on one side. Flip with a spatula and cook the second side until golden. Place on a baking sheet and keep warm in a 200°F oven while frying the remaining cakes.

4. Serve hot.

Fried Moroccan-Style Fish

Fried chicken for Chanukah pops up on menus for at least one of the eight nights of festivities. I thought it would be a good idea to combine the tradition of frying some sort of animal protein with a nod the Crypto Jews of Portugal, and the spices of North Africa and the Middle East—where the first Chanukah was celebrated. The addition of turmeric gives the fish a golden glow like that of an oil lamp.

SERVES 8

3 pounds thick, white fish fillets, such as cod or pollock, cut into 1½-inch-wide strips

Grated zest and juice of 1 lemon

1 garlic clove, mashed through a press

1 tablespoon dried thyme

1 rounded tablespoon ground cinnamon

1 rounded tablespoon ground cumin

1 teaspoon Aleppo pepper flakes

1 tablespoon ground turmeric

¼ cup extra-virgin olive oil

2 teaspoons salt

1½ cups all-purpose flour

Neutral oil, such as canola for frying

4 large eggs, well beaten

Lemon wedges for garnish

NOTE: *Don't be alarmed if, toward the end of frying, the oil becomes foamy. You might clean the oil between batches with a skimmer.*

1. Combine the fish, lemon zest and juice, garlic, thyme, cinnamon, cumin, Aleppo pepper flakes, turmeric, and olive oil in a large bowl. Cover and refrigerate for at least an hour and up to 2 hours.

2. Remove the fish from the refrigerator 1 hour before frying. Add the salt to the fish and stir thoroughly to coat the pieces, then place the flour in a shallow dish and thoroughly dredge each piece of fish with the flour.

3. Fill a skillet halfway full of neutral oil and heat over medium heat until a wooden chopstick inserted in the center of the oil has bubbles around it. Dip four or five pieces of the flour-coated fish in the beaten eggs and place into the skillet. Cook for 1 to 1½ minutes on each side, using the chopstick to flip the pieces. Remove them with a wire-mesh strainer, shake away any excess oil, and drain on paper towels. Keep warm in a 200°F oven while frying the remaining pieces in batches of four or five. Serve hot and garnish with lemon wedges.

Scratch any scholar of Jewish food—or fish and chips—and they will likely tell you that when Thomas Jefferson visited London and ate fried fish, he called it "'fish in the Jewish fashion." You will also learn that fried fish was a favorite of the Portuguese Crypto Jews who ate fried fish on Fridays, and saved some to eat cold on the Sabbath so they didn't have to cook. In 1863, Joseph Malin, an Ashkenazi immigrant to England, opened the first "chippy" shop in London. Who would ever guess that British comfort food supreme is really Jewish food?

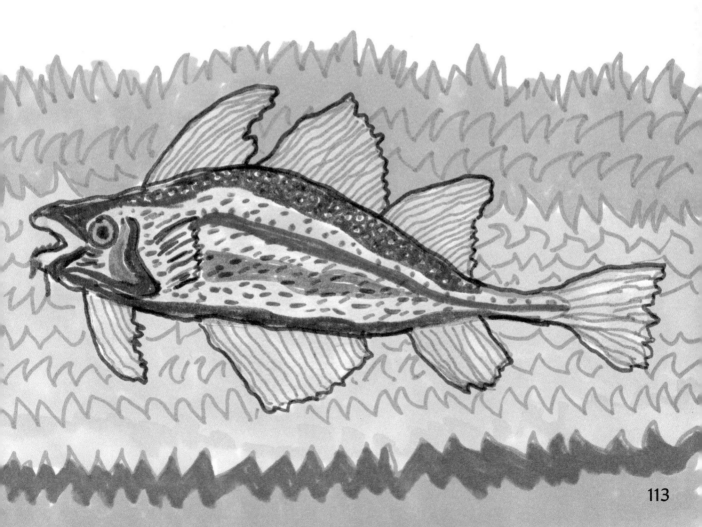

Roast Breast of Duck
with Sour Cherry Sauce

SERVES 4 TO 6

CHERRY SAUCE

½ cup sweet red vermouth

½ cup brandy

1 heaping teaspoon finely chopped fresh rosemary

2 cups pitted sour cherries

1 cup freshly squeezed orange juice

¼ cup orange marmalade

2 tablespoons unsalted butter, cut into chips

Salt

DUCK

6 duck breasts

¾ cup brandy

1 teaspoon freshly ground black pepper

1 teaspoon salt

There's a long-forgotten Italian-Jewish tradition of serving a goose on Chanukah. A bit easier, equally celebratory, and certainly less fatty are these fatty enough, pan-roasted duck breasts, accompanied by a savory cherry sauce made with those sour cherries that you so wisely froze from the summer harvest.

MAKE THE SAUCE

1. Combine the vermouth, brandy, rosemary, and cherries in a medium-large, nonreactive saucepan over medium heat. Cook until the cherries are tender, about 15 minutes, lowering the heat, if necessary, to avoid boiling.

2. Use a slotted spoon to transfer the cherries to a bowl. Add the orange juice and marmalade to the pan. Cook until the sauce is reduced by about half and is slightly syrupy, 15 to 20 minutes.

3. Add the cooked cherries to the sauce. Continue to simmer. Add the butter, piece by piece, stirring after each addition. Remove the sauce from the heat and set aside.

MAKE THE DUCK

1. Remove all but a 1½-by-2-inch piece of fat from the duck breasts. Score the fat on the duck in a crisscross pattern.

2. Place the duck breasts, fat side down, in a large, heavy-bottomed skillet over high heat and cook for 8 to 10 minutes, or until the fat is golden and crisp. Turn them over and brown in the rendered fat for 2 minutes. Pour off all but a tablespoon of the fat from the skillet (save for another use, such as roasting potatoes). Add the brandy, pepper, and salt. Lower the heat to medium-low and simmer until the meat is done to your taste. Duck tastes very good rare.

3. Taste the cherry sauce for seasoning, add as desired, and reheat over medium heat.

4. Place the duck breasts on a serving platter. Pour the pan juices over the top. Add the cherry sauce to cover. Serve immediately.

The kosher goose, and its fine-feathered relative, the duck, gained fame in Italy when the Jews of the northern and central regions of the country cured them to resemble the renowned prosciutto made from a pig's thigh or hind leg. The rich flesh of geese and ducks, made into *prosciutto d'oca* and *d'anitra*, respectively, satisfied—and continues to satisfy—a craving for the *treif* cured meat.

Chiacchiere

SERVES 6 (UNLESS YOU CAN'T KEEP YOURSELF AWAY FROM THEM)

3 cups all-purpose flour, plus more if needed and for dusting

3 tablespoons sugar

½ teaspoon baking powder

Pinch of salt

2 large eggs

8 tablespoons (1 stick) unsalted butter, at room temperature

3 tablespoons grappa, or another eau de vie (I use cherry eau de vie) marsala, white wine, etc.

Zest of 1 lemon (about 1 teaspoon)

Oil for frying (I use canola)

Confectioners' sugar for dusting

Tempting as it is to try to make sufganiyot, I opted for something more in my lane, and is a bit easier to produce; *chiacchere* ("gossip," in Italian) are crunchy, melt-in-your-mouth thin strips of fried dough made for Carnevale (Carnival) time in all the regions of Italy. Every bar and restaurant will bring you, without asking, a plate of chiacchere and one of *frittole*, which actually resemble little sufganiyot, their spongy dough filled with jam or pastry cream. Think of *chiacchere* as a refined version of a state or county fair's offering of fried dough. Friends who tasted my version couldn't believe they were fried.

1. Combine the flour, sugar, baking powder, and a pinch of salt in a large bowl and whisk together.

2. Add the eggs, butter, grappa, and lemon zest. Thoroughly mix the ingredients. The dough may seem sticky at first; keep kneading until a smooth dough is achieved. You may need to add a bit more flour.

3. Heat 2 inches of oil in a large, deep skillet over medium-high heat. Line a tray or cookie sheet with double layers of paper towels.

4. Place the dough on a floured work surface. Cut into four equal pieces. Use a floured rolling pin to roll out each piece into as-thin-as-possible strips that measure about 4 inches wide.

5. Use a pie crimper to cut ¾- to 1-inch-wide strips. Pile the strips on a plate. Repeat with each piece of dough.

6. Fry the chiacchiere in batches (do not overcrowd), using a wooden chopstick to flip them around the oil until golden, about 90 seconds. Use a wire-mesh strainer to transfer them to the paper towels to drain.

7. Repeat until all the strips are cooked. Generously dust the cooled chiacchiere with confectioners' sugar. They will get crunchy as they cool.

8. If you have leftovers, store them in a paper bag. They're good for up to 2 days.

Sufganiyot, the much-anticipated Chanukah jelly doughnut, was already an ancient preparation when, in the 12th century, Maimonides (the Sephardic Jewish scholar of the Talmud) quoted his father, Rabbi Maimon ben Yosef, "One must not make light of the custom of eating *sofganim* [fried fritters] on Chanukah. It is a custom of the Kadmonim [the ancient ones]." Sufganiyot are particularly popular in Israel, where the puffy pastry's name was changed from its Polish progenitor, *paczki* (in Yiddish, *ponchiks*) to its present name, which means "spongy dough."

Tu B'Shevat

CHAPTER EIGHT

Tu B'Shevat

The moon
pregnant with every hope
for a healthy springtime birth,
greets us with her radiant fullness.

From the Rabbi

Susan: *What is Tu B'Shevat?*

Zoe: It has been seven weeks since our last holiday of Chanukah, the darkest time of the year for those of us living in the Northern Hemisphere. Since then, our days have been lengthening, offering their hopeful promise of spring. In Israel, the rainy season is winding down and the arrival of Tu B'Shevat signals the beginning of spring. It is said that on this day, the sap, that nutrient-rich blood-life of the trees, awakens from its winter sleep and restarts its yearly flow. We humans, after a long winter, peel off our outer layers of protection and are drawn to a deep exhale. Then, as our lungs expand with our next inhale, our senses follow suit. All this foretells of a restart and of new possibilities. What better model of this is there than the tree herself, she who the Torah calls The Tree of Life.

Tu B'Shevat is an anomaly of a holiday because it wasn't created as such. "Tu" isn't even a word but, rather, a number, and "Shevat" is the name of a month; Tu B'Shevat therefore is the 15th of (the Hebrew month of) Shevat. Any holiday occurring on the 15th of their respective month gives cause for an extra portion of joy because the moon is guaranteed to be full.

On this holiday, we celebrate and honor the tree, every single one of them and all the magnificent fruits that they bring forth. This, however, is a relatively new way to express the transformation of this day's original function. It is in the Torah, our most sacred of texts, that we learn about most of our holidays. However, it is in the Mishnah, a collection of writings of the Oral Torah, the partner to the written Torah, where we learn of Tu B'Shevat. It is referred to as the Rosh HaShanah (Head of the Year) of the Tree.[51]

This was the day when the tithe on the produce of each tree was calculated. Fruits harvested prior to this date were deemed taxable for the previous year, and harvested after were for the new year. This was Tu B'Shevat in the days when the temple stood in Jerusalem. Like many observances, after the destruction of the temple, there was nothing to do or calculate anymore on this date. It wasn't until the 16th century, when the Kabbalists of Safad studied the ancient mystical teachings of Kabbalah, that Tu B'Shevat was transformed into a holiday. They saw this as Rosh HaShanah of the Tree, a time of spiritual reawakening for people just as trees emerge from their winter dormancy. This became a day of hope, reminding us that although we cannot see life in a wintertime tree, we know it is alive, preparing to burst forth with all its potential. The Mishnah says, "One whose deeds are greater than his wisdom, to what is he compared? To a tree with many roots and few branches, which all the storms in the world cannot budge from its place."[52] The Kabbalists taught that the cosmic tree has its roots in heaven and that the Divine sap flows downward through its trunk and branches to imbue us with her energy and inspiration. Imagine preparing for this holiday and expecting to come out the other side personally transformed. As our days lengthen, we, too, are reminded of the Divine that flows within us and, like the bud on the tree, our full potential is just waiting to blossom forth.

I know Rosh HaShanah is the New Year, but I also heard you say Passover is one, too. Now, you say Tu B'Shevat is a kind of New Year. Why?

The Mishnah states that Tu B'Shevat is one of four New Years in our tradition. At first, this may sound odd, but we also have different new years within our secular calendar. January 1 begins our calendar and tax year. The fiscal year used by organizations for financial planning, budgeting, and reporting their finances varies according to the companies or businesses and can start at the beginning of any month. Our federal government's fiscal year has its own timetable and runs from October 1 through September 30. The (first) Jewish New Year, Rosh HaShanah, the most familiar one, which occurs on the first of the Hebrew month of Tishrei, is designated as the calendar New Year. The second, Tu B'Shevat falls next on our calendar as the Rosh HaShanah of the Tree. The third Jewish new year occurs on the first of Nissan, corresponding to when the Hand of God released our ancestors from the bonds of slavery and therefore this month is

---

51   Mishnah: Rosh HaShanah 1:1
52   Pirkei Avot 3:17

considered as the birth of the Israelite nation. The Torah calls for this month to be first when we count our festivals, which is why Passover always occurs in the first month and was also the New Year for the reigns of Jewish kings. The last new year occurs on the first of Elul and was the New Year for the tithing of cattle.

When I think of a seder, I think of Passover. Why do you lead a seder on Tu B'Shevat?

The Kabbalist created a *Tu B'Shevat* seder, which like the Passover seder, involves four cups of wine; however, in this seder each one symbolizes one of our seasons. Today, many people refer to this day as the birthday of the trees. We relish the beauty, and bless, taste, and savor each fruit of the Shevat HaMinim (Seven Species) named in Torah, once staples of our ancestors in Israel. "For Adonai your God brings you into a good land, a land with brooks of water, of fountains and depths springing forth in valleys and hills; a land of wheat and barley, and vines and fig trees and pomegranates; a land of olive trees and honey."[53] To make a more abundant seder, we welcome as many fruits and nuts as possible, dividing them into groups corresponding to each season. The Kabbalists taught that as we eat each piece of fruit, we are aiding in the healing of the trauma from the Garden of Eden where both Adam and Eve ate from the forbidden Tree of Knowledge. Imagine if this were so! I don't even think we know how drastically that one story has affected generations of those who have grown up with it. Imagine if we really could heal that past and re-create something new from that wound. Could it be that every taste we experience actually brings us closer to our return to that original garden, Gan Adin, that place within us where there is no divide?

Beginning with winter, the season of our celebration, we bless and eat fruits that, like those of us who must bundle up during this season, have a hard shell or inedible skin on the outside but are edible inside. These are such fruits as coconuts, almonds, walnuts, pistachios, and all other nuts, oranges, pomegranates, and etrogs, the citrus fruit similar to a lemon that is central to our festival of Sukkot. We drink white wine or juice, the color of winter. As we crack open the shells of the fruit, we aspire to break free from the hard places that bind us and endeavor for our inner essence to be revealed.

Just as we shed our layers of clothing when springtime arrives, we bless and eat fruits that have a soft outside but a hard pit inside. These might include dates, olives, apricots, and plums. We drink white wine or juice with a splash of red, symbolizing the blush of springtime. We reflect on the seeds within us that call to be planted and nurtured in the outer world. What longs to burst forth in us?

---

53 Deuteronomy 8:7–8

With summertime and the freedom associated with this season, we eat fruits that are fully edible, such as grapes, figs, berries, apples, and pears. We drink red wine or juice, aspiring to realizing our full potential.

For autumn, when our harvest is complete, we do not eat fruits, but instead reflect on the completion of the yearly growing cycle. We pause and give thanks for all that has been and all that is. We bless and drink red wine or juice with a splash of white to symbolize the changing season and our turning once again toward winter.

We are left with two grains to give thanks for, barley and wheat. For the first, I like to serve a delicious, hearty soup, not unlike the recipe Susan has included (Tanabour, page 126) in this chapter. For the second—a long, braided challah—see Susan's recipe on page 54, and acknowledge the partnership with God that this bread symbolizes.

"When God created the world, God made everything a little bit incomplete. Instead of making bread grow out of the earth, God made wheat grow so that people might bake it into bread. Instead of making the earth of bricks, God made it of clay so that people could become God's partner in the task of completing the work of creation and sustaining our earth."[54] When we say the blessing before eating bread, we praise and thank the Creator for bringing forth bread from the earth. This reminds us of the ongoing invitation to our holy partnership. Just as we make bread from wheat and wine from grapes the Holy One has given us, the Holy One needs us to fulfill the Divine plan and we need The One's help in order for us to fulfill our destiny. Bottom line, we need each other.

Tu B'Shevat is a stunning example of how our traditions have changed and adjusted with the times. Just as a day of taxation was transformed through a spiritual lens into an exquisite and sensuous holiday, we, too, have the hope to transform ourselves into something greater than we could have imagined. As we look out from our winter landscape, we look forward to next month's Purim full moon, and the following one when our springtime festival of Passover begins. This is a time of building energies, as seen reflected in the heavens as the moon swells and recedes each month.

Rabbi Simon said, "There is no plant without an angel in Heaven tending it and telling it, GROW!"[55] If we can embrace that idea then we might sense an inkling of the wealth of love and unending support there is for each one of us from the unseen world. Imagine with that in mind; "Man is like a tree planted by streams of water, that yields its fruit in its season, and its leaf does not wither."[56]

---

54 Midrash
55 Midrash Genesis Raba 10:7
56 Psalm 1:3

If we are likened to a tree, then what are the fruits we have each born? What fruits have we taken for granted? What produce have we allowed to wither and decay? What seeds have we been unable to nurture and what seeds are laying wait just to be cared for so that they may blossom? If we are like a tree, then I want to be that inverted tree the Kabbalist spoke of. I want to gather my sustenance into my roots from the heavens. I want to draw that nourishment down through my body and out through my arms and legs so that every action is heavenly directed.

May we all plant seeds, not only for ourselves and our loved ones, but for future generations. May the seeds that our words plant, the ones we say to others and to ourselves, be good ones. May the seeds that our actions produce be healthy. May we inspire one another to be our best selves. May the Holy One bless us with the inspiration, strength, insight, support, and discipline for us to realize our greatest selves. May we remember to thank the One for all that is provided.

I leave you with one of my favorite Tu B'Shevat stories from the Talmud:

Honi HaMe'agel (Honi the Circlemaker), a Jewish scholar from the first century BCE, was out walking and saw a man planting a carob tree. Honi asked, "How long will it take for this tree to bear fruit?"

The man answered, "SEVENTY YEARS!"

Honi kept asking questions. "Do you think you will live another seventy years?"

"No, but I'm not planting this for me, but for the next generation and the one after that! I found carob trees in the world because my ancestors planted them for me, so I too plant these for my children."[57]

---

57 Babylonian Talmud Tractate Ta'anit 23a

Simon bar Yochai (Simon, son of Yochai) taught,

"If you are holding a sapling in your hand
And someone says that The Messiah has drawn near,
FIRST PLANT THE SAPLING and then go and greet The Messiah!"[58]

Commentary: Completing a task that involves providing for the well-being of the next generation takes precedence over rushing to greet the Messiah! This surely tells us how important our tradition views caring for our children and our children's children. May it be so! A favorite tradition of this holiday is to plant a tree in Israel.

58 Talmud Seder Nezikin, Avot d'Rebbe Natan 31b

From the Cook

This exquisite celebration of the seven ingredients repeated in the Bible as ones that sustained our ancestors—wheat, barley, grapes, figs, pomegranates, olives, and dates—couldn't come at a more appropriate time. We're slogging through the depth of a dark winter in real need of colorful distractions (unless you live in the Southern Hemisphere). We can make all this food with long-shelf-life ingredients—with the exception, perhaps, of fresh pomegranate arils—just as our ancestors did.

Fattoush

SERVES ABOUT 4

3 to 4 firm ripe tomatoes, or an equal amount of cherry or grape tomatoes

2 to 3 young cucumbers

1 medium onion, or 3 scallions

1 to 2 small hot peppers

½ cup chopped fresh mint leaves

⅓ cup olive oil

Finely chopped peel and juice of 1 large lemon

½ teaspoon pomegranate molasses

1 to 2 stale or toasted pita breads

1 garlic clove, split

Arils of 1 pomegranate, or ½ cup tart dried fruit

Salt

The subtitle of this recipe might be "Pita and Pomegranate Salad." The salad is particularly delicious when pomegranates are in season and their burst-in-your-mouth, tart arils (seeds) add so much to the salad. I, however, make it all year-round and substitute either dried tart cherries or dried cranberries for the pomegranate arils, and add ½ teaspoon of pomegranate molasses to dress it. This is just the kind of salad you'd find at an Israeli breakfast. Like much of the food in the Israeli kitchen, this salad has the Palestinian kitchen as its origins. Early Jewish settlers adopted this practice for the same reasons as the Palestinians did originally—they were poor, and fresh vegetables were readily available and cheap.

1. Chop the tomatoes, cucumbers, onion, and peppers, transfer them to a large bowl, and sprinkle with the mint leaves. Add the chopped lemon peel and lemon juice. Add the oil with a generous amount of salt and mix well.

2. Split the pita(s), rub with the open end of the split garlic, tear into bite-size pieces, and toss into the salad. Add the pomegranate arils and mix well. Add salt to taste.

3. Serve immediately.

Tanabour

YOGURT BARLEY SOUP WITH FRESH MINT
AND PARSLEY

SERVES 6 TO 8

4 tablespoons (½ stick) unsalted butter

1 teaspoon olive oil

1 large yellow onion, chopped finely

¾ cup dried barley, soaked overnight in 1 quart water

5 cups chicken or vegetable stock

3 cups plain whole-milk or low-fat yogurt (*not* nonfat)

1 large egg

¾ cup finely chopped fresh flat-leaf parsley

½ cup finely chopped fresh mint, plus whole leaves for garnish

Salt

Straight out of the Armenian kitchen, this silky soup is filled with nubs of barley—quite possibly the oldest, and most adaptable, grain in the world as it grows in frigid highlands and scorching deserts—and fragrant fresh herbs. It satisfies when served hot in chilly weather, or at room temperature, or cold in sweltering heat.

1. Melt 3 tablespoons of the butter in a large, heavy-bottomed, nonreactive saucepan with the olive oil over medium heat. Add the onion and cook until very soft, about 7 minutes.

2. Drain the barley, then rinse and drain again. Add to the saucepan along with 4 cups of the stock. Bring to a simmer, then cook over low heat until the barley is tender, about 50 minutes.

3. Whisk together the yogurt and egg in a medium bowl until smooth. Stir it into the soup. Cook over low heat for 10 minutes. Do not boil. Add the remaining cup of stock.

4. Meanwhile, melt the remaining tablespoon of butter in a small skillet over medium heat. Add the parsley and mint and cook until wilted, about 1 minute. Stir the herbs into the soup and simmer for 2 minutes to blend the flavors. Season with salt as desired.

5. Serve with a fresh mint leaf as a garnish in each bowl.

Carrot and Pomegranate Salad

SERVES 4 TO 6

4 cups grated carrots

¾ cup fresh pomegranate arils (from about 1 large pomegranate)

¼ cup finely chopped fresh flat-leaf parsley

¼ cup coarsely chopped sunflower seeds

¼ cup coarsely chopped roasted almonds

Juice of 1 lemon (just under ¼ cup)

⅓ cup coconut milk

1 teaspoon fine sea salt

1 teaspoon ground cinnamon

Moses had to assure Jews, departing from Egypt—where pomegranates grew in abundance—that they would find them again in the Promised Land. The ball-shaped fruit, filled with jewel-like arils, is protected with leathery skin. The arils contribute a sharp, sweet-tart flavor to whatever they're added to. In this recipe—from the Jewish kitchen of Kerala in South India—the arils add just the right contrast to the sweet carrots. The coconut milk provides creaminess without relying on dairy products.

1. Combine the carrots, pomegranate arils, parsley, sunflower seeds, almonds, lemon juice, coconut milk, salt, and cinnamon in a large bowl and toss together.

2. Marinate for 1 hour before serving.

Baked Radicchio *with Wheat Berries, Chickpeas, Raisins, Olives, and Feta*

MAKES 10 STUFFED, BAKED RADICCHIO LEAVES

4 cups water, plus more if needed

1 cup rinsed wheat berries

2 tablespoons olive oil, plus more for baking dish

One 15-ounce can chickpeas, drained and rinsed

6 scallions, outer layers and ends trimmed, white and pale green parts chopped

10 cured Moroccan olives, pitted, chopped (about ¼ cup chopped)

½ cup raisins

1½ cups crumbled feta

⅓ cup chopped fresh flat-leaf parsley

Salt (optional; I didn't use, as I think the olives and feta add enough)

20 medium to large radicchio leaves

¼ cup dry white wine or vermouth

This Tu B'Shevat recipe contains three of the seven celebrated ingredients—wheat, raisins (grapes), and olives—mentioned in the Bible. It's also another way to stuff a vegetable, a method so loved by all the kitchens of the Jewish Diaspora. Stuffing vegetables is a way of preparing a meal ahead of the Sabbath, or holidays, so you won't have to work on the actual day of the celebration.

1. Heat the water in a large saucepan over medium-high heat. Add the rinsed wheat berries. Bring to a boil, then lower the heat to medium. Cook the wheat berries, stirring occasionally, until tender but still chewy (you may need to add more water), about 90 minutes. Remove from the heat and let cool.

2. Heat the oven to 400°F.

3. Heat the olive oil in a medium skillet over medium-high heat. When the oil is hot, add the chickpeas. Cook until they begin to appear crispy, about 10 minutes. Add the scallions and toss to combine. Remove from the heat.

4. Transfer the cooled wheat berries to a bowl. Add the chickpeas, olives, raisins, 1 cup of the feta, and the parsley. Taste for salt and add, if desired.

5. Use a bit of olive oil to oil a large ceramic or terra-cotta baking dish. Cover the bottom of the dish with a thin layer of the wheat berry mixture.

6. Make 10 stacks of two radicchio leaves each. Place about ¼ cup of the wheat berry mixture in the cavity of each stack. Fold in the sides of the leaves, wrapping them around the wheat berries, and place, seam side down, atop the wheat berry layer in the baking dish. The first row should be placed along the top half of the width of the dish. The tops of the bundles of the second row will overlap the bottoms of the first row a tiny bit.

NOTE: *Add freshly chopped vegetables and hard-cooked eggs to the leftover wheat berries for a tasty breakfast or lunch.*

7. Sprinkle the wine over the radicchio. Cover the dish with parchment paper or foil. Bake for 15 minutes.

8. Remove the parchment or foil. Increase the oven temperature to 450°F. Sprinkle the bundles with the remaining ½ cup of feta. Bake until the cheese melts and is slightly browned, 15 to 20 minutes. Serve immediately.

I consider chickpeas to be the gateway to my interest in food and subsequent addiction to it. Chickpeas weren't on my childhood menus, but my favorite book, *All-of-a-Kind Family*, by Sydney Taylor, was. There is a passage in the book that I've read hundreds of times because it so clearly sets the scene for a carefully selected snack. The all-of-a-kind were a Jewish family with five girls living on New York City's Lower East Side. Shopping day meant each of the girls got a penny to buy a treat from a street vendor. Although most of the girls chose candied fruit, Sarah chose chickpeas from the "good-natured" chickpea vendor. "Everyone watched as he fished out the peas. First, he took a small square of white paper from a little compartment on one side of the oven. He twirled the paper about his fingers to form the shape of a cone and then skillfully twisted the pointed end so the container would not fall apart. He lifted the wagon cover on one side revealing a large white enamel pot. The steam from the pot blew its hot breath on the little girls' faces so they stepped back a bit while the peas were ladled out with a big soup spoon. The wagon cover was dropped back into place and the paper cup handed over to Sarah. The peas were spicy with pepper and salt, and how good they were!"

Red Wine Poached Pears
Filled with Pomegranate Seeds and Mascarpone

SERVES 6

1 liter full-bodied red wine

2 to 3 cups water

½ cup sugar

2 cinnamon sticks

Small cheesecloth packet of 4 whole cloves and 4 cardamom pods

6 Bosc, Anjou, or Comice pears with stems intact, but peeled and cored from the bottom up (opening should be about 1½ inches in diameter and about 1 inch deep)

1 cup heavy cream

4 ounces mascarpone

Arils from 1 pomegranate (about ¾ cup)

End your meal with these mascarpone-stuffed poached pears. The encore appearance of pomegranate arils in the recipe serves to highlight the reverence that Jews hold for the fruit. According to the Bible, pomegranates represent righteousness, knowledge, and wisdom.

Just be sure that the food that precedes the dessert is pareve—or switch out the heavy cream and the mascarpone in favor of coconut milk yogurt.

1. Pour the red wine and 2 cups of the water into a large, nonreactive saucepan over medium-high heat. Add the sugar, cinnamon sticks, and spice packet. Bring to a boil, then immediately lower the heat to just above a simmer. Add the pears, and more water, if necessary. The liquid should cover them a little more than halfway.

2. Cook the pears, turning them over every 15 minutes or so, until a tester easily passes through them, 1 to 1½ hours.

3. Use a slotted spoon to remove the pears from the poaching liquid. Place them in a baking dish to cool. Remove the spices from the liquid. Increase the heat beneath the saucepan to reduce the liquid to a syrup. A syrup is achieved when the liquid falls off the edge of a spoon in drops. The whole process should take 20 to 30 minutes. Remove from the heat and let cool a bit. Stir in the cream. Transfer to a glass container and refrigerate.

4. Place the mascarpone in a small bowl. Stir in ½ cup of the pomegranate arils. Use a teaspoon to fill the cored opening of each of the pears with the mixture. Cover and refrigerate until ready to serve.

5. To serve: Place a pear on a dessert dish. Use a soup spoon to coat the pear with about ¼ cup of the sauce. Garnish with pomegranate arils.

Soft Date and Chocolate Cake

MAKES A 9-INCH ROUND CAKE; IF CUT INTO VERY SMALL PIECES (IT'S RICH), COULD SERVE 18 TO 20

2 large eggs

¾ cup sugar

1 cup 00 flour

1 teaspoon baking powder

½ teaspoon salt

2 tablespoons honey

2 ounces unsweetened chocolate, chopped coarsely

5 ounces raw almonds, chopped coarsely

9 ounces Medjool dates; save 3 for garnish, coarsely chop the rest

2 tablespoons milk, orange juice, or plant-based milk, like oat or almond (I use oat milk)

Unsalted butter for cake pan (optional)

Garnish: unsweetened whipped cream, crème fraîche, mascarpone, ice cream, coconut milk yogurt, or Plant-Based Milk Pouring Custard (page 26), etc.

The Bible tells us a tall tree pointed toward heaven was what served as the compass that led the Jews, exiting Egypt, to the Land of Milk and Honey–Israel. The tree was a date palm. Date palms are considered the oldest fruit-bearing tree in the history of civilization. Their fruit was made into syrup (*silan*) and the tree juices were fermented into wine (surprisingly, the crushed dates produce a kind of licorice flavor–something like Arak).

1. Heat the oven to 350ºF.

2. Whisk together the eggs and sugar in a large bowl to get a frothy cream. Carefully incorporate the flour, baking powder, salt, and honey.

3. Add the chocolate, almonds, and dates to the egg mixture, adding the milk, if necessary, to make the dough more workable (I do).

4. Line the bottom of a 9-inch round cake pan with parchment paper, or butter the entire pan (go with the paper if making pareve). Add the mixture to the pan and level it. Cut the remaining dates into four pieces each and place them in a decorative circle in the middle of the cake.

5. Bake the cake until a tester inserted in the middle comes away clean, about 40 minutes.

6. Remove the cake from the oven and let rest for about 5 minutes. Remove from the pan and place on a serving plate to cool.

7. The cake is very dense and sweet. Serve it in small slices, perhaps accompanied with one of the suggested garnishes.

8. This cake keeps well tightly wrapped in plastic or parchment paper for a few days.

131

Ginger Crostata *with Fig Jam and Fresh Figs*

SERVES 8

JAM

1½ cups Brown Turkey
  (the ones that grow in
  more northern climates)
  or Mission figs, stems
  removed and discarded,
  chopped coarsely

¾ cup sugar

2 tablespoons water, plus
  more if needed

1 tablespoon freshly
  squeezed lemon juice

1 cup water, if using
  semidried figs

PASTRY

2½ cups all-purpose flour,
  plus more for dusting

½ cup sugar

Pinch of salt

¼ cup chopped crystallized
  ginger

8 tablespoons (1 stick) plus
  6 tablespoons (¾ stick)
  unsalted butter, cut into
  bits

1 large egg

8 to 9 medium fresh or
  semidried figs, stems
  removed and discarded,
  quartered

GLAZE

5 teaspoons sugar

5 teaspoons port

Figs, in Judaism—a star in Tu B'Shevat festivities—are among the most revered symbols as an augury of good will and good health. The fig, a beautiful purple, black, or green soft-skinned fruit with about a gazillion tiny seeds occupying its rosy interior, has inspired poets, artists, and cooks since it was first discovered—maybe in Turkey or maybe in northern India. Its famous perfect, graphic good looks and uniquely delicious flavor have given it the opportunity to travel far and inhabit the most extraordinary places.

I lived with a fig tree planted in a container on my New York City terrace (I wrapped it in multiple layers of straw and burlap every winter), on the property of my one-time home in the Piemonte region of Italy, and in my sister, of blessed memory, and brother-in-law's Nantucket garden.

This crostata uses figs in two ways: as a jam filling and as fresh fruit topping. Fresh figs aren't always available. Semidried ones are second best and can fill in as needed.

MAKE THE JAM

1. Combine the chopped figs, sugar, water, and lemon juice in a nonreactive saucepan over medium-high heat. Bring to a boil, then lower the heat to a simmer. Stir almost constantly until the sugar has dissolved and a jam is achieved, 10 to 15 minutes. Add more water as needed. Big lumps in the jam are fine. Remove from the heat and set aside to cool.

MAKE THE PASTRY

1. Combine the flour, sugar, and salt in a food processor. Pulse several times. Add the butter and pulse until fully combined. Add the egg and chopped crystallized ginger. Pulse until the dough forms a ball on the blade. Divide in half, form into two balls, and wrap in waxed paper or plastic wrap. Chill one ball for at least 30 minutes. Freeze the other for another easy, last-minute jam tart.

2. Heat the oven to 350°F.

3. Remove the pastry from the refrigerator and let it come to room temperature, about 15 minutes. On a lightly floured work surface, roll out into a circle large enough to cover the bottom and sides of a 10-inch fluted tart pan with removable sides. Press the pastry into the pan and trim away any excess. Prick the bottom. Fill with the fig jam, spreading evenly with a rubber spatula.

4. Arrange the quartered figs in even circles on top of the jam.

MAKE THE GLAZE

1. Whisk together the sugar and port until the sugar dissolves. Use a pastry brush or spoon to completely cover the fig topping.

2. Bake until the crust and figs are golden, 30 to 35 minutes. Remove from the oven and let cool on a rack.

3. Remove the pan sides. Consider serving the tart slices with Plant-Based Milk Pouring Custard (page 26).

Micah 4:4 "Every man shall sit under his grapevine or fig tree with no one to disturb him." What a thought. What power.

CHAPTER NINE

Purim

In all her fullness,
she is ready to pop
with every aspect of us
wrestling inside of her.
What a party!

From the Rabbi

Susan: *I've heard there is a day of fasting that proceeds this raucous holiday of Purim. What is this about?*
Zoe: Taanit Esther (the Fast of Esther) is observed on the 13th of the Hebrew month of Adar, one day before Purim. However, if Purim falls on a Sunday, the fast day does not occur on Shabbat and is moved to the preceding Thursday. This is done so as not to decrease the joy of preparing for and celebrating Shabbat. The most popular reason we are taught to fast on this day is to be in solidarity with the memory of Queen Esther's fast.

I wonder how many people realize when they say, "The whole megillah," that it references the story of a woman, Queen Esther. Why is her story so important?
Queen Esther and her predecessor, Queen Vashti, both risked their lives standing up for what they believed in amid this topsy-turvy holiday. It is these strong women who anchor our Purim story.

The narrative unfolds in Megillat Esther (the Scroll of Esther, found in the Tanach,[59] whose evening's chant ignites this raucous holiday. Thankfully, the category "drinking parties" does not exist in Guinness World Records; however,

---

59   Hebrew Bible

just imagine one lasting for 180 days! This is how our story begins. The host, King Ahashverosh, who threw this extravaganza for his ministers and servants, wanted to impress them with his great wealth and status. He added seven more days of revelry for the people he reigned over. On the last day, the king called for his wife, Queen Vashti, to present herself to the men and show off her beauty. She refused to capitulate and was, at the very least, banished from the kingdom with the loss of status and possessions. The Talmud, however, relates that she was killed on the very day she defied her husband.[60] In no time, a search for a new queen ensued throughout his vast territories, and soon, a group of potential young maiden queens had been assembled. Esther was chosen from among them. Her assent to the throne carried a strong message from the king to the men of his kingdom, that no woman would have the upper hand in marriage.

Under strict guidance from Mordechai, who was her cousin/adoptive parent and a real *mensch* (a person of integrity and honor), Queen Esther kept a rather significant secret from her husband. He had no idea she was a Jew!

Esther received horrific news. At the bidding of the newly appointed prime minister, Haman, the king had signed a decree to annihilate all the Jews, men, women, and children.[61] This was a manifestation of an ego-crazed Haman who expected everyone to bow down before him. No matter what he tried, he was unable to get Mordechai to do so. However, with barely any effort, Haman persuaded the king that Mordechai and his kind were troublesome and needed to be erased.

Now, the fact that Queen Esther had never revealed her Jewish identity to her husband put her in a terribly fragile position. The king had no idea that his signing the decree was a signing of his wife's death warrant. For three days, she fasted, and asked her people to do the same, before mustering all her courage, strength, and chutzpah (extreme self-confidence) to come before the king. It is said that the queen's fasting was a form of praying for Divine assistance and intervention to save her people from destruction. As no one was permitted to enter the king's inner sanctum without invitation, she easily could have been killed instantly if her sudden appearance had been met with displeasure.

Fortunately, because otherwise we wouldn't be here to tell this story, Esther found favor in the king's sight, so much so that he offered her the golden scepter that was in his hand.[62] With poise and cleverness she invited the king and Haman to a party, and at that party to a second one, and it was there that she unveiled her identity. King Ahashverosh stood tall for his wife when he heard

---

60   Talmud, Megillah 12b
61   Esther 3:13
62   Esther 5:2

the shocking news. Although the Pur (lottery) had already been chosen and the date for killing all the Jews had been well advertised, the king signed a new decree allowing the Jews to defend themselves. Great battles and many deaths ensued. Haman and his 10 sons were all hanged on the gallows that Haman built for Mordechi, who subsequently rose to take Haman's position of vizier. Talk about the tables being turned.

It is quite fascinating that in this story the queen is called both Hadassah and Esther. "Hadassah" is derived from *hadas*, the myrtle tree, one of the four plant species biblically commanded to be waved in thanksgiving during the festival of Sukkot.[63] I love this subtle connection to another holiday because it reminds me that although our holidays can be stand-alone days, they are at their core profoundly connected to one another. Esther's name Hadassah holds within it the seed of joy that I believe she got to experience by fulfilling the reason she was chosen to be queen. She does, after all, save her entire people and becomes the hero of our story. The Talmud explains she was given this name because the righteous are called myrtles from a quote from another biblical book, Zechariah.[64] On the other hand, "Esther" means "hidden." Her two names reflect her outer righteousness (Hadassah) and inner, Jewishness (Esther). Her faith, however, is not the only hidden aspect of Purim.

It is customary not only for children but for willing adults to wear masks and costumes disguising their identities. Is it not also an opportunity to delight in revealing some aspect of ourselves we usually work hard to keep covered up? I'll never forget the time I watched a rabbi performing in a Purim spiel,[65] remove his shirt and pants to reveal a Superman-like costume, cape and all, boasting a huge Hebrew letter shin sewed onto this top. Or the time my friend Jerome, of blessed memory, then an octogenarian with a long flowing beard, noticeable belly, and over 6 feet tall, dressed up as Esther as he wore a pink tutu and carried a wand. Or the year I dressed as a male rabbi wearing a *shtreimel*, the traditional large fur hat worn by some Chassidic men, and *tzitzit katan* (little *tzit tzit*). These are special knotted fringes attached to the corners of an undershirt-like garment worn by men. I wore a white shirt and suit and told the women I could not shake their hand, much less offer or receive a hug or kiss. For me, pretending to be a man for a few hours was thought-provoking and a tremendous amount of fun. It is also something that I wouldn't do in a traditional community where the laws of modesty are a way of life and crossdressing could cause someone to make physical contact with someone they never

---

63   Leviticus 23:40
64   Zechariah 1:8
65   Yiddish, meaning a Purim play

would normally touch. This is all indicative that on this day, things are just not as they seem. The greatest concealment of all is God's name, as it is nowhere to be found in the Book of Esther. Song of Songs, which we read during our next festival of Passover, is the only other book in the Tanach (Bible) where God's name is absent.

You've mentioned that there are many mitzvahs associated with this day. What are they?

The story of Purim is one I always found troubling and off-putting largely because of the excessive violence. Only because of my daughter's childhood love and fascination with this holiday, and my desire to form a positive connection with it so I could full-heartedly celebrate with her, did I take a deeper dive in to the story. It is a complex one that contains layers upon layers of symbolic meaning, much like the entire Tanach. You may have heard the adage that all our holidays can be summed up as, "They tried to destroy us, we survived, let's eat." Although one of the mitzvahs of this day is to have a *mishteh* (feast), it is about so much more than that. We are commanded to give to the poor, traditionally a gift of money called Matanot La'Evyonim. We gift at least one friend two ready-to-eat treats called Mishloach Manot and to listen to the whole megillah! This reflects such wisdom on behalf of our sages who created these traditions.

At Temple Israel of Catskill, we have engaged our entire community by taking a creative approach to these directives, and each year we do something different. Here are a few examples.

- We made gift bags filled with toiletries for residents of local nursing homes and assisted living facilities.
- We made gift bags filled with crayons, puzzles, and toys for children in our local hospital.
- We raised money for our local Muslim community.
- We raised money and made gift bags of school supplies for the Jewish community in Uganda and sent a tallit (prayer shawl) for each person becoming bar or bat mitzvah.

We don't have to have a holiday fully figured out to be able to be a joyous participant. We can uplift ourselves and others with the pure joy of fulfilling the mitzvahs and let the unfolding happen as it will, in time. I can tell you that for me, I went from not relating to this holiday to loving it, but I'll also share that this did not happen overnight.

What is this thing about increasing joy? How's that accomplished?
The Talmud says, "When Adar enters, joy increases."[66] We draw our strength and joy from the story of Purim and the characters who enacted it whose message is one of hope and triumph. We are shown that, even at a time when it seems there is no way out, behind what we see is an opening—there is light at the end of the tunnel. This message of hope is the story of the strength and survival of the Jewish people. This is the joy of Purim.

One way my joy gets increased during Adar is to actively seek out new ways to express the holiday of Purim. A few years ago, I worked with Arm-of-the-Sea Theater when we were commissioned by the Museum of Jewish Heritage in New York City to create a Purim spiel. The theater artists made fantastic puppets, I wrote the music, and together we crafted the words of the Purim spiel. Their style of puppet making is to create these huge, colorful papier-mâché heads that the actors wear over their heads. For our production, they also created these marvelous handheld stick puppets of the young maidens who had been sought out for the role of replacement queen. All the figures are musicians or dancers and I have used them every year in whatever way Purim is celebrated at my synagogue. We have had author Paul Cooper, who wrote a Purim spiel involving the adults and kids in our community. My favorite thing to do is to lead a service, really a spoof on davening (praying), that somehow honors it at the same time. This is commonly done in synagogues around the world on Purim.

In recent years, our community has been blessed to have musician, author, and producer Henry Sapoznik translate and offer dramatic readings of *Megillat Esther* in Yiddish. The whole idea is to keep it fresh and exciting, and at our little shul, we do everything we can think of to do just that.

> The Talmud says, "When Adar enters, joy increases." We draw our strength and joy from the story of Purim and the characters who enacted it whose message is one of hope and triumph.

Is it true that revelers are supposed to be so inebriated on Purim so that the good guy and the bad guy are indistinguishable?
I think this addresses the most remarkable opportunity of this day. As someone who doesn't drink, it is important for me to say that there are many ways to reach alternate states of mind without imbibing substances. The idea is we can certainly get to the place the rabbis are talking about without alcohol, if we choose.

---

66   Talmud, Taanit 29a

In our tradition, the concept of separating things is monumental. It organizes our lives in life-affirming ways, helping us live effectively and healthfully. The order and times of our prayers clearly delineate day from night; the separating of milk and meat makes us conscious of the source of our food and the humanity with which we consume it; and learning what to do and what not to do so that we may choose life by discerning the ethical choices as the Torah instructs. Let's not leave out that when we make Havdalah (separation), the Saturday night ceremony that marks the completion of Shabbat, we offer a blessing giving thanks for that separation. During our morning blessings, we give thanks for the ability to distinguish between day and night. Oy, the list is truly endless. Let it suffice to say that making distinctions is truly a cornerstone of Jewish life. Now, we have this outlandish holiday where we are asked to dissolve our ability to distinguish knowing right from wrong, of knowing who is good and who is evil. How can it be that we are asked to get so inebriated that we cannot distinguish between Mordechai and Haman?

Mordechai, older, kind, protective, menschlich Jewish man, and Haman, psychopathic, anger-monger, murderous narcissist, are the two extreme characters in this story. But there is also the easily swayed, weak-minded Persian king; his first older and more experienced Queen Vashti who risked her life standing up for herself; and his young virginal Queen Esther who carries a big secret and saves her people. We have the guards who plotted to kill the king; Haman's wife, symbolic perhaps of his feminine side; and their 10 sons, reminding us how easily good or evil can increase. What a crazy bunch of characters for a story! We naturally tend to identify these characters as either good or bad and often as "other," certainly not anything like us. But just try this on for size: Imagine that they all live inside each of us. Imagine that every time we have the urge to oppress someone else, we see our inner Haman. Or when we feel kind and protective, recognizing that our inner Mordechai is alive and well. How about when peer pressure gets the best of us? Could we have a bit of the king acting up within us? What about when we stand up for what we know is right and take a big chance by doing so? Is your inner Queen Esther speaking up and being heard?

Herein lies the exquisite hidden beauty of the story of Purim and how it can give us one phenomenal leg up to self-reflect and prepare ourselves for what is coming next, our festival of freedom and liberation, Passover. The Baal Shem Tov taught that if we are reading the Book of Esther as history, we are missing the boat. It is meant to be read as something totally relevant for us today. In this way, Purim becomes a vehicle for change and transformation much like Rosh

Hashanah and Yom HaKippurim, literally "like Purim." May we find joy and release in both days.

Is it true that when the Messiah comes, this will be the only holiday celebrated?

This is so radical, and yet, this is what the sages teach. Not only that but that the entire Tanach (Bible), except for the Book of Esther, won't be needed! Some say that Chanukah as well as Purim will be the only two remaining holidays. The reason given is this: Everything in our Torah, and the point of all our holidays, is to make ourselves better, to be the best we can be, to make ourselves vessels to receive the Divine and reflect the Holy of Holies back into the world. When Mashiach comes, we will have realized how to do this. We will have learned how to care for each other and how to live in peace with ourselves and one another. Perhaps then we will be living embodiments of the Sh'ma, of Oneness. Maybe it will become clear that Mordechai and Haman are a part of the One, as is everyone on the planet. If the holidays exist to bring us to this place, then we won't need them anymore. We will be in a constant state of gratitude and joy. Perhaps then the topsy-turvydom of the Book of Esther will allow us to laugh and rejoice in our own and everyone's safety and freedom. We won't have to hide anything in our closets or behind closed doors. There probably won't be doors. All will be, Sh'ma Yisrael: Adonai Elohaynu, Adonai Echad (Listen, Israel: Adonai is our God, Adonai is One. All will be One).

In the case of a leap year, called Shanah Me'uberet, literally a pregnant year, we have 13 months in our year. This occurs 7 times within a 19-year cycle. The result is the exquisite balancing of the lunar and solar cycles. We end up having months Adar I and Adar II and always celebrate Purim in Adar II.

From the Cook

Before I began this journey of Jewish holiday discovery with Zoe, I used to wait, drooling, for the arrival of Purim, which was announced by the appearance of platters, and platters of hamantaschen piled high in pyramids displayed in the large window of the late-lamented Moishe's Bakery located on Second Avenue in my East Village, New York City, neighborhood. The triangular pastries were meant to resemble—according to what you choose to believe—the hat, ear, or pocket of the villain of the Book of Esther, Haman.

Moishe's hamantaschen—with their crumbly shortbreadlike base, folded into their filling-revealing shape—contained a variety of sweet mixtures: prune or apricot lekvar, or *mohn* (poppy seed paste).

I was thrilled to attend my first real Purim celebration at Temple Israel of Catskill where the Book of Esther was performed by imaginatively costumed Cantor Suzanne and Rabbi Zoe. One read the whole Megillah in Yiddish, and the other in just enough English to make it understandable. All this took place as the youngest members of the congregation, in their own creative drag, pranced back and forth in front of the reading rabbis, holding up numbered signs to announce each new chapter of the book, much as prizefight announcers let the crowd know which round is starting. Extra jollity was assured with the croaking sound of *groggers*, Yiddish for "rattles," used to cancel out the villainous Haman's name every time it was mentioned in the story. Fortunately, for our entertainment, his name was mentioned often.

My admiration for Purim was sealed when I began to make some food to fit the occasion. Purim arrives at a time when I'm waiting for fresh spring produce. You know, for something that's green to relieve a winter's table filled with nearly monochromatic ingredients. Aside from the grand variety of soft-leafed, fresh herbs grown by local farmers in their hoop houses, I can count on spinach, and on the overlapping seasons of the still available, tart-sweet varieties of citrus and tropical fruits that I use with alacrity to spark up many dishes.

A milk pudding called *sutlage*, flavored with orange blossom or rose water, might be found in the selection of dishes from Turkey, and countries of the Balkans. An Italian Jewish dish, mentioned in Edda Servi Machlin's outstanding book *The Classic Cuisine of the Italian Jews*, called *taglionini alla crosta alla Bolognese* (a crunchy pasta topped with Bolognese sauce), was common on the author's Purim table.

As my education of Purim developed, I was heartened to learn that Queen Esther was a vegetarian when she was married to King Ahashverosh and lived in the palace. She chose vegetarianism to keep her unaccepted Jewish religion a secret. Instead of explaining why she wasn't eating meat dishes—because either the meat was butchered in a way inconsistent with kosher law, or the meals may have been presented with both meat and dairy dishes on the same plate—she simply chose an all-vegetable diet. An all-vegetable diet does not exclude dairy-based food. Vegetables are pareve, a neutral food, anything that's not meat or dairy. For Purim, you can mix dairy and vegetables, no problem. In fact, Purim is sometimes referred to as a dairy holiday.

Spinach and Ricotta Kreplach *Floating in a Lake of Saffron and Ginger Broth*

SERVES 4 TO 6

BROTH

2 tablespoons olive oil

¾ cup chopped yellow onion (about 1 medium onion)

2 garlic cloves, chopped finely

1 cup diced carrot (¼-inch dice)

2 celery stalks peeled and chopped into ¼-inch dice (about ¾ cup diced)

½ pound waxy yellow potatoes cut into ¼-inch dice (about ¾ cup diced)

1 heaping tablespoon grated fresh ginger

½ teaspoon saffron threads

¾ teaspoon salt

¾ teaspoon freshly ground black pepper (I use a pinch of hot pepper flakes)

6 cups water

Handful of celery leaves (from the heart of a bunch) for garnish

Kreplach is the Yiddish word for "stuffed pasta." *Pelmeni*, ravioli, and wontons are some other words for stuffed pasta. Traditionally kreplach are stuffed with chicken, then served in their broth. With this recipe, I honor Queen Esther with kreplach stuffed with spinach, lemon-scented ricotta, and chives, then serve them floating in a highly flavored vegetable broth. The broth of my imagination conjures food that may have been served in the Persian court of both queens, Esther and Vashti, two of the brave protagonists of the story.

Save some kreplach to shallow-fry to golden crispiness, and then serve them as an appetizer alongside caramelized onions and a dollop of sour cream.

MAKE THE BROTH

1. Heat the olive oil in a nonreactive stockpot or large saucepan over medium-high heat. Add the onion and garlic and sauté until the onion is translucent but hasn't taken on color.

2. Lower the heat to medium and add the carrot, celery, potatoes, ginger, saffron, salt, and pepper. Add the water. Cook until the vegetables are soft but not mushy, 30 to 40 minutes. Remove from the heat and set aside.

KREPLACH (MAKES ABOUT 40; FREEZE WHAT YOU DON'T USE)

2 teaspoons olive oil

5 packed cups spinach, rinsed, tough stems removed

8 ounces whole-milk ricotta

1 teaspoon grated lemon zest

4 teaspoons chopped fresh chives or finely chopped scallions, white and pale green part only

1 teaspoon salt

1 large egg yolk

One 12-ounce package wonton skins

MAKE THE KREPLACH

1. Heat the olive oil in a medium skillet over medium-high heat. Add the spinach leaves and toss to coat with the oil. Cook until the leaves are just wilted, a couple of minutes. Remove from the heat and set aside.

2. Combine the ricotta, lemon zest, chives, and salt in a medium bowl and stir well.

3. Coarsely chop the wilted spinach and stir into the ricotta mixture.

4. Place the egg yolk in a small bowl. Use a fork to gently beat it. Lay a wonton skin on a clean surface. Place a heaping teaspoon of the ricotta mixture in the center of the skin. Use a narrow brush—or, more easily, your finger—to draw a line with the egg along the left and bottom sides of the skin. Fold over the skin to make a triangle, pressing firmly on the sides to carefully enclose the filling. Set aside. Repeat the process until the filling is finished.

5. Cook the kreplach in gently boiling water for 3 to 4 minutes before scooping out with a wire-mesh strainer and adding to the hot vegetable broth.

6. Heat the broth for another minute or so. Taste for seasoning and add as desired.

7. Add three or four kreplach to each soup plate, then cover with the broth. Garnish with celery leaves to serve.

145

Assorted Citrus and Mango Salad *with Mint, Scallions, Black Olives, and Feta-Pomegranate Molasses Drizzle*

SERVES 6

DRESSING

¼ cup extra-virgin olive oil

2 teaspoons pomegranate molasses

½ teaspoon salt

¼ teaspoon Aleppo pepper flakes

SALAD

4 Cara Cara oranges, peeled and cut into sections (see Note)

2 pink grapefruits, peeled and cut into sections (see Note)

2 ripe mangoes, peeled and cut into ¼-inch slivers

⅓ cup Kalamata or cured Moroccan olives, pitted and chopped coarsely

½ cup crumbled feta

¼ cup coarsely chopped fresh mint leaves, plus whole leaves for garnish

Citrus salads are made in southern Mediterranean and North African countries, where citrus fruits grow in abundance in months when a good majority of us are shivering through chilly winter weather. This salad, with its tart, sweet, sour, salty, and herbaceous flavors, is the kind of starter that acts as an aperitif for dishes to come. Its bright colors alone are visual reminders of a celebration.

MAKE THE DRESSING

1. Combine the olive oil, pomegranate molasses, salt, and Aleppo pepper flakes in a small bowl. Use a small whisk (one of my favorite kitchen tools) or a dinner fork to stir the ingredients until emulsified. Set aside.

MAKE THE SALAD

1. Arrange the oranges, grapefruit, and mangoes in overlapping circles on individual plates or a large platter.

2. Toss the olives, then the crumbled feta, over the fruit.

3. Whisk together the dressing again. Drizzle over the top of the salad. Sprinkle the chopped mint over the top. Garnish each salad plate with a whole mint leaf.

NOTE: *To peel and section citrus fruit, use a very sharp paring knife to peel away the skin, then the white pith from the fruit. Using the same sharp knife, carefully remove the segments, one at a time, by cutting between the fruit and the membrane. Remove the seeds from the segments. Squeeze the remaining "corpse" for a little juice.*

Spinach Borani

MAKES 3½ TO 4 CUPS

2 tablespoons olive oil

1 medium yellow onion, sliced thinly

1 pound spinach, rinsed, tough stems removed

1 teaspoon salt

2 cups Greek-style whole-milk yogurt or Labna (page 25)

2 medium celery stalks, peeled and sliced thinly into half-moons

⅓ cup toasted walnuts, chopped

¼ cup fresh mint leaves, chopped

Zest and juice of 1 lime

Pinch of Aleppo pepper flakes

To serve: raw vegetables and toasted bread, crackers, or matza

Various historical documents report that *borani*, initially made with eggplant and yogurt, has its origins in ancient Persia. It's been described in many ways: vegetables that are boiled, then mixed with herbs and yogurt; as a salad; a dip; or a spread. Borani traveled to Turkey, where both vegetarian and meat—mostly lamb—interpretations of the dish are made. I like to think that Queen Esther dined on something like this spinach borani. It may be one of my new favorite dishes. I like it spread on toast, topped with a poached egg.

1. Heat the olive oil in a large skillet over medium-high heat. Add the onion and sauté until it becomes translucent. Add the spinach and salt and cook until the spinach has wilted. Remove from the heat and set aside to cool.

2. Place the yogurt in a medium bowl. Add the cooled spinach, celery, walnuts, mint, lime zest and juice, and a pinch of Aleppo pepper flakes.

3. Serve in a bowl, surrounded by raw vegetables, and toasted bread, crackers, or matza to scoop it up. Or as a side to grilled fish or meat, or as part of a selection of appetizers.

During the Purim celebration, I heard the rabbis answer a question about when the Book of Esther takes place. "It was in the days of Ahashverosh ... who ruled from India to Ethiopia." *Aha*, I thought; what a good prompt for finding dishes that not only represent the home of the Persian king, but also the countries prominently named in the Megillah.

Kik Wot *with Spicy Parsley Sauce*

Kik wot, or *kik alicha wot,* could be called the Ethiopian national dish. The history of Jews in Ethiopia is at least 15 centuries old, when the Beta Jewish community was created by merchants passing through the northern part of the country. Move ahead 1,500 years, to when the Beta community, who had long suffered from religious persecution, migrated to Israel with help from the Israeli military, first in Operation Moses, then Operation Solomon. They brought their iconic recipe for a yellow split pea stew with them. In true Ethiopian style, this dish should be served with *injera,* a spongy, sour bread that's ripped into pieces and used as a utensil to scoop up the stew. I thought that the split peas might benefit from a finishing sauce that includes peppers, preserved lemons, and herbs. It does indeed add kick to the kik.

SERVES 6 TO 8

KIK WOT

1½ cups uncooked yellow split peas

2 medium yellow onions, chopped finely

3 large garlic cloves, minced

1 tablespoon grated fresh ginger, or more to taste (I like the sharpness ginger brings to the dish so I add 2 tablespoons)

⅓ cup neutral oil, such as canola

1 tablespoon ground turmeric

2 cups water, plus more as needed

1 teaspoon salt

½ teaspoon freshly ground black pepper

PARSLEY SAUCE

2 cups chopped fresh flat-leaf parsley

1 large bunch scallions, chopped, white and pale green part

1 tablespoon finely chopped Preserved Lemons (page 41)

4 teaspoons chopped pickled jalapeño peppers

¼ cup extra-virgin olive oil

Pita bread or rice to serve—or injera, if you can find it

---

1. Soak the split peas for at least 1 hour in warm water.

2. Puree the onions, garlic, and ginger together in a food processor until a smooth paste is achieved.

3. Heat the oil in a large saucepan over medium heat. When the oil is hot, sauté the puree and cook until soft, about 10 minutes, stirring to keep it from sticking to the bottom of the pan.

4. Add the turmeric and stir to combine.

5. Rinse the soaked split peas and add to the pan with the 2 cups of fresh water, plus the salt and black pepper. Cover, lower the heat to low, and simmer, stirring until the peas are soft, about 20 minutes. You may need to add more water.

6. While the peas are cooking, put together the parsley sauce: Combine the parsley, scallions, preserved lemons jalapeños, and olive oil in a medium bowl and stir thoroughly.

7. Gently heat the peas before serving. Add a generous dollop of parsley sauce to each serving to swirl through the dish. Serve with pita, rice, or injera.

Cochin Biriyani

Biriyanis are rice dishes, made all over India, which can be mixed with chicken, lamb, fish, or vegetables. A biriyani is typically served on festive occasions. The Cochin Jews think that their biriyanis are the most flavorful because they use coconut milk to enrich the dish, instead of yogurt, to avoid mixing dairy with meat. A Cochini biriyani also benefits from the addition of acidic tomatoes and fragrant fennel seeds.

SERVES 6 TO 8

- 2 quarts water
- 1 tablespoon white vinegar
- 3 cardamom pods, smashed
- 4 whole cloves
- ½ teaspoon fennel seeds
- 1 cinnamon stick
- 1 teaspoon salt
- 2 cups uncooked basmati rice
- 1 cup unsweetened coconut milk
- 2 teaspoons garam masala
- 1 teaspoon ground turmeric
- 2 tablespoons neutral oil, such as canola
- 1 yellow onion, chopped coarsely
- 1 large garlic clove, chopped finely
- One 1-inch piece fresh ginger, grated
- 2 cups chopped fresh tomatoes (I use cherry tomatoes)
- 2 tablespoons chopped fresh mint
- 2 tablespoons chopped fresh cilantro
- Garnishes: ¼ cup fried cashews, ¼ cup raisins

1. Combine the water and vinegar in a stockpot over medium-high heat. Make a cheesecloth sachet with the cardamom pods, cloves, fennel seeds, and cinnamon stick. Add it to the water along with the salt. Bring to a boil, then lower the heat to medium and cook for 20 minutes.

2. Remove the sachet and add the rice. Cook the rice until al dente, 15 to 25 minutes, depending on the freshness of the rice. Drain and set aside in a bowl.

3. Combine the coconut milk, garam masala, and turmeric in a small bowl. Set aside.

4. Heat the oil in a large skillet over medium heat. Add the onion and garlic and sauté until the onion is caramelized. Add the ginger and the coconut milk mixture. Simmer for 5 minutes.

5. Pour the mixture over the cooked rice and toss to combine.

6. Add the tomatoes and fresh herbs and toss to combine. Taste for seasoning and add as desired.

7. Serve, hot or warm, topped with the garnishes.

Pistachio-Crusted Hamantaschen *Filled with Apricot Butter Made with Last Summer's Fruit*

MAKES 30 TO 32 HAMANTASCHEN

12 tablespoons (1½ sticks) unsalted butter, at room temperature

⅔ cup sugar

1 large egg

¼ cup lightly salted, finely chopped pistachios

2¼ cups all-purpose flour, plus more for dusting

1 teaspoon brandy, plus more if needed

Apricot Butter (page 198) from last summer, removed from freezer

Ever since I started my hamantaschen love affair at Moishe's, I've been thinking about ways to create a version of the pastry that I could call my own. The path that I took to get to this recipe began with apricot butter that I made one summer with local Hudson Valley fruit. I froze batches of it to pull out of the freezer—just as I do with other summer fruit—when the dark winter months need a bit of jazzing up. Then, I saw Purim on the calendar. I had my hamantaschen filling. Hmm, why not pastry with nuts embedded in it? More to the point, why not pistachios that would add their bright green dots of color and a bit more fat to the already butter-rich pastry? Why not, indeed. It's a holiday, after all.

I bake the pastry for just two or three minutes more than you might be accustomed to, because I like the way the crust gets extra crispy and the apricot filling gets sticky.

1. Cut the butter into small pieces and place in a large bowl.

2. Add the sugar to the butter. Use an electric mixer (be careful of flying pieces) or two wooden spoons to cream the butter and sugar together until light and fluffy.

3. Add the egg, pistachios, and brandy to the bowl. Beat again until creamy and the ingredients are well combined.

4. Sift the flour, then measure it again. Add 2¼ cups to the mixture.

5. Mix until a crumbly dough is achieved. Remove from the bowl and knead on a clean work surface until a smooth ball is achieved. Try not to overwork the dough, which will only result in tough pastry. If the pastry seems too dry, add a bit of liquid—brandy or water—until the dough

seems elastic enough for rolling. If the dough is too wet, knead in some extra flour.

6. Pat the dough into a flat disk and wrap in parchment or waxed paper. Refrigerate for at least 3 hours and up to overnight.

7. To bake the hamantaschen: heat the oven to 350°F. Remove the dough from the fridge. I like to start rolling the disk while it's still in loosened paper. Take the partially rolled-out dough and place it on a floured work surface. Roll into a ¼-inch-thick disk. If the dough cracks, use your fingers to pull the dough together. Continue to roll until you can get the dough just a bit thinner. Use a 3-inch-diameter biscuit cutter to cut out circles. Place the circles on nonstick baking sheets (or ones lined with parchment paper). Keep cutting until just scraps remain. Pull together the scraps, roll out again, and cut some more circles. Continue to do this until there is little to none left.

8. Put a teaspoon of apricot butter in the center of each circle. Don't overfill your pastries, or they may crack while baking and spill the filling.

9. Make the traditional hamantaschen shape by tightly pinching together the circle in three equidistant spots. You should've created a shape that resembles a three-cornered hat, with the apricot butter peering out of the center.

10. Place the hamantaschen-filled baking sheets in the oven, one sheet at a time, and bake for 15 to 20 minutes, until the hamantaschen are cooked through and golden (I like a longer baking time to create a crispy crust). Begin to check your hamantaschen after 10 minutes of baking time.

11. Remove from the oven and let cool on a wire rack. Store in cookie tins–if you save them like I do–or in airtight containers. They keep well for about 5 days.

Lemon-Limoncello Olive Oil Cake

MAKES ONE 9-INCH CAKE; SERVES ABOUT 10

1¼ cups olive oil, plus more for pan

2 cups all-purpose flour

1¾ cups sugar

1½ teaspoons flaky sea salt

1½ teaspoons baking soda

1 teaspoon baking powder

1 cup oat milk

¼ cup plain coconut yogurt

3 large eggs

2 teaspoons grated lemon zest

¼ cup limoncello liqueur

Optional additions to the batter: 1 cup pitted sour cherries, 1 cup blueberries, or 1 cup raspberries; if you add fruit to the cake, replace the limoncello with Luxardo for the cherries, cassis for the blueberries, and Chambord for the raspberries

Olive oil cake's ancestry can be found in the southern part of the Iberian Peninsula. The Sephardic Jews of Spain may have created cakes just like the ones that are encountered on today's dessert and café menus. I created this version of the cake to serve to my lactose-intolerant friends. The use of olive oil instead of butter in the batter solves one of the problems. I substituted plant-based milk and coconut yogurt for the often added cow's milk. The result was a moist cake with a perfect crumb.

The cake is not seasonal produce dependent; I like to serve it with another lactose-free dessert, Roasted Rhubarb and Orange Dairy-Free Custard (page 183) when rhubarb is in season in late spring, during Lag B'Omer.

1. Heat the oven to 350°F. Rub olive oil around the bottom and sides of a 9-inch-diameter by 2-inch-high round cake pan and line the bottom with parchment paper.

2. Whisk together the flour, sugar, salt, baking soda, and baking powder in a large bowl.

3. In a separate large bowl, whisk together the olive oil, oat milk, coconut yogurt, lemon zest, and limoncello until just combined. Expect a thin batter.

4. Pour the batter into the prepared cake pan. If adding fruit to the cake, add it after the batter has already been poured into the cake pan. Gently stir it in and hope that it doesn't sink to the bottom. Alternatively, you might add half of the fruit at the beginning and the other half spread over the top when the cake is about 10 minutes from finishing baking.

5. Bake on the center rack of the oven for 55 minutes to an hour, until the top is golden and a cake tester inserted into the center of the cake comes out clean. Remove from the oven and let the cake cool on a wire rack for 30 minutes.

6. Run a knife around the edge of the cake pan, invert the cake onto the rack, peel off the paper, and let cool completely before serving.

7. As this is a moist cake, it will keep for up to 5 days wrapped in parchment or waxed paper.

CHAPTER TEN

Pesach

Proud as she could be,
with her third full moon holy day in a row,
she is ready
to birth our people into freedom.

From the Rabbi

Susan: *Why is this night different from all other nights?*
Zoe: During Pesach, known in English as Passover, we retell our people's journey from slavery to freedom. In the Passover seder, we enact the most unique of rituals by eating the symbols of that journey as our narrative unfolds. We are taught that the Divine Hand took our ancestors out of bondage and just as they were helped, we, too, must extend our hand to others who are not yet free. Although we rejoice with our freedom, we know that we are not truly free until everyone is free.

    This night is truly unique from all other nights. Passover is our people's birth story filled with intimate details of struggle, exceptional labor pains, and the miraculous birth of a free people. For some, Passover can be the most exhilarating holiday; for others, even its approach can cause massive internal seismic activity as the list of to-dos is over the top. On this night, we have more rituals and symbols filling our table than we have at any other holiday. Before we even get to that night, we have thoroughly cleaned and rid our homes of *chametz* (any foods that are leavened), symbolizing our puffed-up selves, our egos. Instead, during Passover, we eat matza, the bread of our affliction. Purim prepares us to look within, to hold up a mirror and take an accounting of ourselves. On this night, as we recall our people's birth pangs, we anticipate a transformation like theirs, knowing we are once again being offered the chance to begin anew as The Torah defines this festival as beginning the New Year. The trick, and there is one, is to keep reminding ourselves that even if we get distracted by the details, we want at all costs to avoid drowning in them. It's important to remember we must start where we are, which means we may not be able to do everything. The truth is that every holiday has the potential to enslave us or liberate us and Passover is the ultimate example. Even doing one mitzvah for the holiday is a great blessing.

The Torah instructs us to observe this festival in the springtime beginning on the 15th of Nissan, another full-moon celebration.[67] In the Diaspora, it lasts for eight days, and in Israel and for Reform Jews, seven. In Israel, one seder is held on the first night whereas in the Diaspora, seders are held on the first two nights. *Seder* means "order" and the Haggadah outlines the 15-step progression of the Passover seder, containing prayers, blessings, stories, and songs. Although there is a tremendous variety of Haggadahs (Haggadot in Hebrew), published throughout the world, they all are incomplete because they lack our voice. It is essential that we bring the seder alive with our own offerings.

Asking "Why is this night different from all other nights?" is central to the Passover seder and found in every Haggadah from the traditional to the most liberal. We call this "Mah Nishtanah Halailah Hazeh" (The Four Questions). This liturgy originated in the Mishnah (Oral Torah), and is over 2,000 years old. Customarily, before the meal, the youngest person who can ask these questions does so in Hebrew or whatever language they can manage it in. It used to be that this was recited by a parent after the meal and was more like four statements than four questions. This is another example of how our tradition is alive and always evolving.

Several years ago, hosting a joyous community seder in our synagogue, we used every plate, glass, and chair, and wondered what we would do next year. A wonderful congregant, David Vipler, who owns the Catskill Golf Resort, generously offered that we hold our next seder there—and what a gift this has been. At a recent golf course seder, I invited everyone who came from another country to say, "Why is this night different from all other nights?" in their language of origin. It was deeply moving to hear this spoken in over 20 languages, including Hindi, Korean, Ukrainian, Russian, Urdu, Tagalog, Swedish, Italian, Spanish, and French. After a moment of silence just taking in the beauty of it all, we sang the question in Hebrew, weaving together the yearnings of people from around the globe.

One of the reasons this night is so different is that it is such a relatable holiday. We are taught, "In every generation, each person is to look on themselves as if they came forth personally from Egypt."[68] We are asked to imagine that we had been slaves and been redeemed by the Divine. Contemplating this sets the stage for what unfolds in the Haggadah.

---

67 Leviticus 23:5
68 *Talmud,* Pesachim 116b

Our story takes place in Egypt where the villainous Pharaoh ruled cruelly over the Israelites. Having an entire people in bondage wasn't enough. As the Hebrews grew in numbers, for fear of them overpowering the Egyptians, Pharaoh decreed a horrific order for the midwives to drown all the baby boys in the Nile River. Is this not reminiscent of Purim, where the evil king signed a decree to kill all the Jews? In this story, the Voice from within the burning bush, the "I Am That I Am," told Moses to go to Pharaoh and tell him, "Let my people go!" When Pharaoh refused, the Ten Plagues brought disaster and destruction upon the Egyptian people. After the final plague where the death of every firstborn Egyptian was killed, Pharaoh released the slaves. They grabbed their dough that hadn't had time to rise and followed Moses into the unknown. When Pharaoh's anger welled up, he sent his troops after his former slaves. When the Red Sea miraculously split open to reveal dry land for the Hebrews to cross onto, the Egyptians followed them. Once the Hebrews had safely passed over to the other side (thus, the festival's name), the sea came together and drowned all the Egyptians. The Talmud tells a story that when this happened, one of the angels wanted to sing a song of praise. God said, "My creatures are drowning in the sea, and you wish to sing a song?"[69] During the seder, we remove a drop of wine from our cup for each plague, decreasing our joy as we recall the suffering of our oppressors.

It is crucial that, when retelling this story, we remember that Egypt is where it took place and symbolizes a place of constriction within us. It would be tragic if in telling our liberation story, we oppressed or marginalized another people by demonizing the Egyptians. After all, in this very story we are told, "Do not oppress the stranger for you were once strangers in the land." The whole reason this holiday is so pertinent is that we all have ways in which we are oppressed and are always in a struggle to become free, whether we are conscious of this or not. The whole ritual of the seder and the observance during the holiday gives us time to look within and identify where we are imprisoned. In Hebrew, the word for "Egypt" is "Mitzrayim," which is translated as "the narrow place." Passover invites us to look within and see our own narrowness. Do we have addictions? Are we in an unhealthy relationship? Are we being abused or are we abusing others? Are we treating others the way we want to be treated? Do we oppress ourselves?

What is the purpose of Elijah's Cup?

A staple on the table is Elijah's Cup, a silent offering for the one who will herald in the Redemption, when Mashiach (the Messiah) will come. "Lo, I will send you Elijah the prophet before the coming of the great and awesome day of Adonai."[70]

---

69   Megilla 10b
70   Malachi 3:23

We fill his cup to the brim and open our door signifying our faith in God. Just as the Holy One protected the Israelites on the evening before the last plague when the Angel of Death passed over the homes painted with blood of the sacrificial lamb, we believe we will be protected now. Differing opinions exist throughout the Talmud and the discussion of whether there should be a fifth cup at the seder is no exception. Some say that this cup is just that. I remember fondly, spying my father sipping from Elijah's Cup when he thought I had gone to bed. That memory always fills me with immense warmth.

What sorts of nontraditional items are added to seder plates? Why?

When I was a child, I certainly never thought of adding anything to the seder plate. After all, it's enough of a challenge remembering what goes on it and why. If any changes are to be made, there would have to be a very compelling reason.

When I came into my Judaism as an adult, something stirred in me when I sighted a yam and an orange on a friend's seder plate. I thought I was witnessing a new tradition being enacted. It turns out, the idea of adding alternative items originated in the Talmud,[71] where Rabbi Huna said that beets and rice could be used to represent the two cooked foods, the roasted shank bone and egg. The lamb bone symbolizes the Korban Pesach (the sacrificial lamb), and the egg, the Korban Hagigah, the other festival sacrifices that were eaten in the temple. It seems these substitutions were allowed for practical reasons because not everyone had access to all the traditional items.

The addition of the orange came about in response to the AIDS crisis of the 1980s. Scholar and author Susannah Heschel, daughter of famed Rabbi Abraham Joshua Heschel, was inspired to place an orange on her seder plate to bring awareness and support to the gay and lesbian communities. Everyone was asked to take a section of the orange, say the appropriate blessing thanking God for the fruit of the tree, and after eating the fruit, spit out the seeds of homophobia. The practice, minus the spitting of the seeds, caught on like wildfire, and subsequently, the orange has come to represent the entire LGBTQ+ community and how vital their inclusion in the Jewish community is. For these reasons, an orange has a permanent place on my seder plate.

We know Passover has a plethora of rituals, so who can imagine wanting to add yet another one? All the fans of the women, that's who. As important a role as Miriam played in the Bible, she isn't once mentioned in the traditional Haggadah and neither are her two brothers. Of course, our story couldn't have unfolded as it did without all of them. Miriam's Cup, filled with water, is a tribute to the prophetess and her gifts to the Israelites. Miriam watched as her mother

---

71 Tractate Pesachim 114a

placed her baby brother in a basket in the river.[72] Pharaoh's daughter saw the baby and took compassion on him, realizing full well he was a Hebrew.[73] Miriam approached her and asked whether she would like her to find a wet nurse for him. When the answer was yes, she brought him to her mother.[74] Pharaoh's daughter named him Moses, meaning "I drew him out of the water." After the miracle of the parting and subsequent crossing of the Red Sea, the whole community sang a song in unison. "And Miriam the prophetess, the sister of Aaron, took a tambourine in her hand; and all the women went out after her with tambourines, dancing."[75] Miriam's Cup represents *mayim chayim* (the living waters), a powerful biblical reference to God.[76] The Midrash says that those living waters filled Miriam's Well, something that accompanied our ancestors and helped sustain them during their desert journey and dried up only after her death.[77] Varying rituals having to do with water have evolved around Miriam's Cup, from filling her cup before or during the meal and drinking or not from that cup. However it is enacted, the cup reminds us of The Living Waters we all long to drink from.

In 1991, when the Ethiopian Jews arrived in Israel, many were starving and/or ill. They were given potatoes or rice, as it was all their digestive systems could handle. After this, potatoes started appearing on seder plates demonstrating solidarity with the Ethiopian Jews.

In recent years, more and more people have been adding their own items to the seder plate, each one symbolizing a group of people who have been oppressed and/or unseen. Placing this food on our plate brings attention to their plight and signifies standing for those people.

For over 10 years, I had the privilege of coleading Passover seders with Rabbi Joanna Katz and Susan Griss, a dancer and choreographer at Bedford Hills Correctional Facility, in Bedford Hills, New York. When Rabbi Joanna first asked me to join her, I was apprehensive about going into a maximum-security prison, but was willing to give it a try because of the great respect and admiration I had and have for her. I figured, worse came to worst, I would go once and never have to return. The seder took place on the Sunday before Passover, and I can tell you, I was thoroughly unprepared for how moved I was meeting the women of Bedford and how powerful the entire experience was. Our presence was greeted with phenomenal appreciation and I found myself feeling very at ease. I loved bringing my accordion and think even security was mildly entertained by searching my

---

72 Exodus 1:4
73 Exodus 1:7
74 Exodus 2:10
75 Exodus 15:20
76 Jeremiah 2:13, 7:13, God is described as "the spring of living water" and Zechariah 14:8 describes Jerusalem as a source of living water.
77 Numbers 20:1

instrument and case. No matter how much I played and sang with all my heart, I always felt I received so much more than I gave from this community of women. I came to rely on the grounding this experience afforded me prior to Passover each year. It set me straight, reminding me of what the core of the holiday was about. Every time I left the facility with the gates harshly clanging behind me, awareness of my freedom and appreciation for it swelled exponentially.

It was at Bedford Hills where I first saw the addition of nonedible items to the seder plate. Rabbi Joanna invited everyone to bring something they wanted to add, a tradition I immediately adopted. There was a lock and a key placed on the plate, something that struck me so deeply that I can still picture it as though it was yesterday. There was also an olive, for peace in the Middle East. Ever since, I place a key for the women of Bedford and all those imprisoned, plus an olive on my seder plate.

This idea fascinates me and I learned of other things people were placing on their plates. Artichokes, symbolizing interfaith marriage that the Jewish people have been thorny about; fair trade chocolate, supporting work standards that prohibit forced labor; and pinecones, bananas, acorns, cashews, and more. When the COVID-19 pandemic began, people started adding beans, symbolizing an inexpensive food that one can easily store, and pineapple, for the first responders, because the fruit has a hard exterior protective of its sweet inside. I added a fortune cookie (they are often made without flour or any grain) to show solidarity with the Asian community and to stand against racism and violence. Now I'm placing chopsticks on my plate in place of the fortune cookie, so there is no worry or confusion over whether wheat was involved. I've added sunflowers for the Ukrainians, and recently a friend brought walnuts (because a whole, shelled walnut resembles a brain) for mental illness awareness. At many vegetarian seders, the roasted lamb shank has been replaced with a roasted yam or beet. What will be on your seder plate this year?

I like that this story features women in pivotal roles. Tell me more.

Having so many women who are strong role models is a cause for celebration, highlighting yet another aspect that makes this holiday so accessible. Moses's mother, Yocheved; his sister, Miriam; the midwives Shifra and Puah; Moses's Midiante wife, Tziporah; and Pharaoh's daughter Batya were all activists who risked their lives speaking and standing for what they believed in. The Talmud teaches, "In the merit of the righteous women, our ancestors were redeemed from Egypt."[78]

---

78   Talmud, Sotah 11b

If Shifra and Puah had adhered to Pharaoh's edict and committed infanticide, we would have no story to tell. Pharaoh had decreed that all Israelite baby boys be drowned. The midwives' commitment to bring life into this world and refuse to follow Pharaoh's rule is a testament to their strength and radical courage. Yocheved, who birthed Moses, kept him safe until she was no longer able to hide him. She had the foresight to place her baby in a basket of reeds at just the right time in just the right current for him to float into the place where Pharaoh's daughter Batya was bathing. Batya, knowing full well the baby she found was a Hebrew, was magnificently defiant. She not only saved but raised this baby as her own under the roof of Pharaoh. The story of Moses's wife, Tziporah, is a wild one.

Moses had just accepted God's call that he should return to Egypt. Tziporah had very recently given birth to their second son when they set out on their journey from Midian. When they stopped at an inn to spend the night, an Angel of God came to kill Moses. Tziporah immediately realized it was because they had not circumcised their baby. She "took a sharp stone and severed the foreskin of her son and cast it at Moses's feet saying, "You are a bridegroom of blood because of the circumcision."[79] This warrior mother redeemed her husband with her child's blood. All these women were fierce and it a blessing we know their names.

---

79 Exodus 4:24

There are many groupings of four that occur during our seder and throughout Passover. There are the Four Questions, the Four Children, the Four Cups of Wine, the Four Promises that God made to us in the Passover story, and the Four Names of the festival. Chag HaHerut (Festival of Freedom), Chag HaPesach (Festival of Passover), Chag HaMatzot (Festival of Unleavened Bread), and Chag HaAviv (Festival of Spring) each highlight different aspects of the festival. The Four Children—The Wise One, The (temporarily) Wicked One, The Simple One, and The One Unable to Ask—symbolize the different ways that we each learn and take in information. In the same way, having different names for our holiday can either be overwhelming and possibly confusing or it can open the door wider for us, giving us more options, more ways to gain entry, more ways to find our own way into the brilliance of Passover.

My seders always include two seder plates: one for use during the meal, followed by a dessert seder plate filled with the delicious sweets of Pesach.

From the Cook

Passover was the first Jewish holiday that I celebrated from a time when I could recognize celebrations that went beyond birthdays, the Fourth of July, and Thanksgiving. My paternal grandparents, in an attempt to nudge their family, especially the grandchildren, toward an understanding of Judaism, made a seder for us. If my memory is accurate—the whole affair seemed full of intense smells—gefilte fish and chicken soup with matza balls—and loud conversation. That was it—for decades (maybe the occasional Chanukah). When I moved to New York City, I made new Jewish friends who considered Passover the most interesting holiday on the Hebrew calendar and prepared seders that turned into rollicking affairs. These parties starred their personal interpretations of the Haggadah—and my addition of dog biscuits to their ceremonial Passover plates as a reminder of the thousands of animals enslaved in shelters who need, and deserve, loving homes. I would alternate years of celebrations with my Socialist friends who made sure that worldwide struggles for justice for all people were included in the evening's read, and another friend who made sure that all the pronouns in their truncated Haggadah were changed from masculine to feminine. Today, they ... would be *they*. Of course, both Passover seder tables were groaning with heaping bowls and plates of delicious food faithful to the Ashkenazi tradition of their ancestors, such as beef brisket, roast chicken, chopped liver, gefilte fish, and coconut macaroons, and the occasional Sephardic and Mizrahi dishes, such as chicken and lemon tagine, or *dafina* (a slow-cooked dish made with beef, potatoes, chickpeas, and lots of spices), bottles of good things to drink, lots of singing, and hilarity—until we finally said, "Dayenu."

Whole Fillet of Salmon Tarragon Mustard–Martini

SERVES 6 TO 8

½ cup Dijon mustard

½ cup dry white vermouth

¼ cup capers

1 teaspoon ground white pepper

Olive oil

One 3½-pound side of salmon, pin bones removed, skinned

10 to 12 tarragon sprigs

Fish as food and as symbols are extensively used in Judaism. However, kosher law prohibits Jews from eating any fish that lack fins and scales. Sorry, no swordfish. It's also prohibited to mix meat and fish in the same cooked dish, although eating them in separate courses is OK as fish are pareve (neutral).

Shortly after my move to the Hudson Valley, I decided to make my first-ever Passover seder as a way of extending myself to my new community of friends—and because I liked the challenge. The table included both Jewish and non-Jewish guests. The menu was created by researching the food of the entire Jewish Diaspora, cooking methods, and in-season produce. Cooking whole fish in parchment paper is a favorite cooking method. The genius of this recipe is in its simplicity of preparation that winds up creating complex flavor.

1. Whisk together the mustard, vermouth, capers, and pepper in a small bowl.

2. Cut a piece of parchment paper to twice the length of the fish. Use olive oil to lightly oil it, then place the salmon in the center of the length of the paper.

3. Cover the fish with the mustard-martini mixture. Pile the tarragon sprigs along the length of the fish.

4. Enclose the fish by folding the paper over from the sides, then the top and bottom, which should meet in the middle. The edges should be made into a small double fold.

5. Place the packet on a baking sheet and refrigerate for at least 8 hours and up to 24 hours. Remove from the fridge and let come to room temperature for 1 hour before baking. Heat an oven to 500°F.

6. To serve: Bake the fish for exactly 11 minutes. The parchment will turn golden brown. Serve immediately. For dramatic effect, place the fish on a serving platter, bring it to the table, and open in front of your guests. Let them be seduced by the savory aroma.

Masa Tiganitas *with Arrope*

SERVES 4

4 to 6 pieces of matza

Milk for soaking matza
(I use plant-based milk;
in particular, oat milk)

4 large eggs

¼ cup (dairy) whole milk–
based or plain coconut
yogurt

⅛ teaspoon freshly grated
nutmeg

¼ teaspoon ground cinnamon

Pinch of salt

Neutral oil for frying (I use
canola oil)

For serving: Arrope
(page 69), maple syrup,
honey, Strawberry-Rhubarb
Sauce (page 185), Amarene
(page 197), chopped nuts,
etc.

The Greek word for fritters is *tigantas*. *Masa tiganitas* are pieces of fried matza. There have been Jews in Greece since at least the fourth century BCE. When the Jews of the Iberian Peninsula were expelled from Spain in 1492, some migrated to a more hospitable Greece. Their fragrant, delicately spiced cuisine found a perfect partner with the ample variety of the Greek produce that greeted their arrival.

This recipe exemplifies true Jewish fusion food when Greek *masa tiganitas* discovered an Iberian sauce, arrope, to make a dish that will surely replace *matza brei* (fried broken matza and eggs) in your Passover repertoire.

1. Stack the whole matzas in an 8-by-8-inch square baking pan, or another receptacle that will accommodate them without breaking them. Cover with the milk. Soak until soft enough to cut, but not to fall apart.

2. Combine the eggs, yogurt, nutmeg, cinnamon, and salt in a medium bowl and mix together until thoroughly blended.

3. Gently remove the softened matza pieces, one at a time, and place on a cutting board. Quarter each piece. Stack them on a plate.

4. Place a large skillet over medium heat and pour enough oil into it to come up the sides by about ¼ inch.

5. The oil is ready when you place a wooden chopstick in the center of the pan and bubbles form around it.

6. Dip the matza squares into the egg mixture, one at a time, and place in the hot oil. A 12-inch skillet should hold about two or three squares at a time. Fry the tiganitas until golden on both sides, about 90 seconds per side. Keep them warm in the oven until ready to serve.

7. Serve with arrope, or any of the other recommended toppings.

Eighteen minutes is key when it comes to baking matza, whether at home or in commercial ovens. The explanation for the firm command is that fermentation takes place swiftly, by the grains'—wheat, spelt, barley, rye, or oats—exposure to moisture for no longer than 18 minutes. Otherwise, the matza dough would become chametz (leavened) and thus unsuitable for Passover. Eating unleavened food for seven days to commemorate the Jews' Exodus from Egypt isn't such a bad deal. Especially when you realize how many ways you can add unleavened food to your menus.

Matza Lasagne *with Spinach and Roasted Butternut Squash*

SERVES 8

One 1½-pound butternut squash, peeled, seeded, and cut into 1½-inch chunks

½ cup olive oil, plus some for pan and drizzling

Flaky salt

8 ounces spinach, tough stems removed, rinsed

½ cup chopped onion

2 teaspoons finely chopped garlic

¼ teaspoon Aleppo pepper flakes

One 28-ounce can peeled plum tomatoes (choose the best quality because they're likely to be preserved in a thick sauce; if the sauce is watery, thicken with a tablespoon of tomato paste)

1 pound whole-milk ricotta

¼ teaspoon freshly grated nutmeg

A few grinds of black pepper

6 matzas

½ cup grated Parmesan

Leaves from 6 flat-leaf parsley sprigs

Is there anyone who doesn't love lasagne with its layers of oozing ingredients complementing one other as they attach themselves to your fork? Here's a recipe that uses sheets of matza instead of pasta, letting you keep up with your lasagne cravings, even during Passover. I used butternut squash for one of the layers as it can be found almost year-round. The flavor of squash diminishes over time—so, you might want to freeze it, peeled and cut into chunks, when it's freshly harvested. Roasting is a good method to coax flavor out of even the most recalcitrant squash.

1. Heat the oven to 350ºF. Line a baking sheet or jelly-roll pan with parchment paper.

2. Arrange the butternut squash chunks, in a single layer, in the pan. Moisten with 2 tablespoons of the olive oil and sprinkle with a pinch of flaky salt. Bake, occasionally flipping the chunks, until all sides are golden, about 30 minutes. Remove from the oven but don't turn the oven off. Mash the roasted squash and set aside.

3. Heat 1 tablespoon of the olive oil in a large skillet over medium-high heat. When the oil is hot, add the still wet spinach and a pinch of salt. Toss to completely coat the spinach. Lower the heat to medium-low and cook until just wilted, 5 to 8 minutes. Remove from the heat and set aside.

4. Place the remaining 5 tablespoons of olive oil in a medium saucepan over medium heat. Add the onion, garlic, and Aleppo pepper flakes to the pan and sauté until the onion is translucent. Use your hands to crush the tomatoes into the pan. Add all of the can's sauce. Simmer for 20 minutes.

5. While the sauce is simmering, place the ricotta in a medium bowl. Coarsely chop the cooked spinach and add to the bowl along with the nutmeg, black pepper, and a pinch of salt. Thoroughly combine.

6. Use a teaspoon of olive oil to lightly oil a 9-by-13-inch baking dish.

7. Assemble the lasagne: Cover the bottom of the dish with 1½ matzas. Spread the mashed squash over the top. Cover the squash with a thin layer of tomato sauce. Cover the sauce with 1½ matzas. Spread the spinach mixture over the top. Cover that with a thin layer of tomato sauce, and then cover it with 1½ matzas. Cover this matza layer with half of the remaining tomato sauce. Cover the top of the sauce with 1½ matzas. Evenly spread the remaining sauce over the top. Sprinkle the Parmesan over the sauce. Sprinkle the parsley leaves on top of the Parmesan. Drizzle olive oil over the top.

8. Bake in the already heated oven until the top is golden and the sides are bubbling. The top of the lasagne should be crunchy—a perfect foil for the almost mousse-like filling.

Tahini-Halva Ice Cream
with Chocolate-Tahini Brandy Sauce

**MAKES 1 QUART
ICE CREAM, 2 CUPS
CHOCOLATE SAUCE**

ICE CREAM

4 large egg yolks

¼ cup sugar

1 cup whole milk or plant-
   based milk (I use oat milk,
   to lighten the ice cream
   a bit)

2 tablespoons tahini

¼ cup brandy

2 cups heavy cream

½ cup crumbled halva (I use
   marbled halva)

CHOCOLATE SAUCE

4 ounces bittersweet
   chocolate, broken

½ cup heavy cream

¼ cup date syrup

¼ cup tahini

2 tablespoons brandy

Ice cream can be the most delicious ending to a Passover seder if you're not serving meat in other parts of the meal. For example, have a fish main course like the one shared in this chapter. A good reason to have ice cream for dessert.

Once you have the method for ice cream making down pat, you can experiment with various ingredients, including in-season fruits and berries. I like this ice cream—and the accompanying sauce—crammed full of sesame seeds in various iterations, tahini, and halva for this holiday because its ingredients have their provenance in the same area of North Africa as the Passover story.

To keep the ice cream from freezing into an impenetrable block, I add alcohol to the mixture.

MAKE THE ICE CREAM

1. Combine the egg yolks and sugar in a medium bowl and whisk together until pale and slightly foamy.

2. Gently heat the milk in a small saucepan, taking care not to scorch it. When the milk appears to erupt around the edges, remove from the heat and whisk in the tahini and brandy. Pour a bit of milk into the egg mixture and stir. Pour the tempered egg into the remaining milk and return the saucepan to low heat. Use a silicone spoon or spatula to stir the mixture up from the bottom until it clings, like a thin custard, to the spoon.

3. Place the heavy cream in a large bowl and set a sieve on top. Pour the custard through the sieve and combine with the cream.

4. Transfer the mixture to your ice-cream maker—a simple, economical electric mixer makes superb ice cream. Let the mixer spin until the mixture resembles ice cream. Add the crumbled halva and spin for another 60 seconds. Remove the ice cream to quart and/or pint containers; freeze immediately.

MAKE THE CHOCOLATE SAUCE

1. Place the chocolate in a small saucepan over medium heat. Watch it carefully as it melts.

2. Add the cream, date syrup, tahini, and brandy. Stir until all the ingredients are fully incorporated and a smooth sauce is achieved. Remove from the heat. Let cool, pour into a glass jar, and refrigerate until ready for use. The sauce will thicken (it's good to use as a spread when thick). To serve, place the jar in a small saucepan filled with simmering water until loosened into a sauce again.

Chocolate Matza Brickle

MAKES 1 HALF SHEET OR JELLY-ROLL PAN, ABOUT 12 BY 16 INCHES

½ pound (2 sticks) unsalted butter

1½ cups packed dark brown sugar

12 ounces semisweet chocolate chips or broken bar chocolate

4 sheets matza

There are as many versions of this addictive treat as there are makers of it. This one is based on a recipe given to me by my friend Sarah Lipsky. The results of this easy recipe produce the best chocolate toffee ever. Believe me, I've eaten infinite amounts of chocolate toffee in my life. You might make little bagsful of the brickle to give to departing seder guests; as my grandmother Dora liked to say, "So you don't get hungry on your way home."

1. Heat the oven to 350°F. Line a half sheet pan or jelly-roll pan with parchment paper.

2. Arrange the matza, in a single layer, on the parchment.

3. Melt the butter in a medium saucepan over medium heat. Add the sugar to the melted butter and stir until combined. Pour over the matza and use a silicone spatula to evenly cover the matza.

4. Bake for 15 minutes. Remove from the oven and spread the chocolate over the top. It will melt into the toffee.

5. Let cool. Break into pieces to serve. Use all your strength to resist eating the whole tray.

Moroccan Mint and Lemon Verbena Tea

MAKES 1 QUART TEA

1 tablespoon ground
  gunpowder or green tea

4 leafy spearmint sprigs

4 leafy lemon verbena sprigs

4 teaspoons sugar, or as
  desired

1 quart boiling water

For garnish: additional bits of
  mint and lemon verbena

NOTE: *Moroccans use the
classic Manchester-shaped pot
("I'm a little teapot" shape)
so they can use the long spout
to pour the tea in a stream
from high above the glass so it
lands in a bubbly swirl.*

I've consumed what seemed like gallons of this tea on each trip to Marrakech. Upon entry to their places of business, the always hospitable Berber, Arabic, and Jewish shopkeepers of the Medina are quick to bring out a silver tray of beautifully decorated little glasses filled with this very sweet tea (I often asked for it *sans sucre*—without sugar), stuffed full of fresh mint and lemon verbena. It's also the tea that accompanied the typically Moroccan breakfast of pancakes, and an afternoon snack of coconut and sesame cookies. The inclusion of lemon verbena is my memory. Add orange blossom flowers, or just mint—spearmint is preferred. You can drink this tea all day, as guests arrive for a seder and at the end.

1. Combine the tea, mint, lemon verbena, and sugar (if using) in a large teapot.

2. Pour the boiling water into the pot. Let the tea steep for at least 3 minutes.

3. Serve in little glasses. Garnish each glass with pieces of mint and lemon verbena.

Eighth Night of Passover

Mizrahi Jews of North Africa celebrate the eighth night of Passover with a holiday called Mimouna. The festivities are a way to thank God for the many blessings and to ensure the upcoming year's crops will be plentiful. Eating in abundance is a directive. In fact, stuffing yourself silly with vast amounts of leavened carbs that have been denied for the past week. The breads of the Yemenite Jews, *malawach* and *jachnun*, are prized for their crispy texture and fatty flavor. Malawach is a flatbread made with thin layers of dough that is then cooked in oil in a skillet. Jachnun is made with thin dough brushed with butter, rolled into a log, and slow cooked, traditionally overnight. Both benefit from a dip in the spicy Yemenite sauce *zhug*, made with parsley, cilantro, garlic, cardamom, coriander, cumin, chilies, and olive oil.

CHAPTER ELEVEN

Lag B'Omer

A few days past her fullness
taking a pause from all she carries,
a celebration erupts
and sparks remove the veil of darkness.

From the Rabbi

Susan: *What does the name of this holiday mean?*
Zoe: The name of this holiday is in code, which is appropriate for this mystical day. To decipher its meaning, we need to know that each letter of the alef-bet, the Hebrew alphabet, has a numerical equivalent. In Hebrew, *lag* is spelled lamed-gimel. Lamed equals 30; gimel, 3. This holiday falls on the 33rd day of the Omer, which lasts for 49 days. However, even though *lag* is written with Hebrew letters, it is not a Hebrew word. This holiday, falling on the 18th of Iyar, is a celebration that includes marking a great rabbi's *yahrzeit* (anniversary of a person's passing) by having massive bonfires, weddings, getting a haircut, and children playing with toy bows and arrows. To have any sense of the why of it all, we need to look at it in context of the entire Omer period.

What is the Omer?
We speak about the Omer as a period of time, and that is not incorrect, as you will see. Actually, it is a biblical grain measurement equaling approximately 43 ounces. During the days when the temple stood, an *omer* of barley, spring-time's first crop, was brought there as an offering on Passover. It can be challenging to picture having only one place to worship, but that is just how it was for our ancestors, as they made arduous pilgrimages to Jerusalem for this and other holy days.

The Torah tells us to commence Sefirat HaOmer (Counting the Omer), beginning on the second night of Passover, and to continue doing so for 49 days.[80] All this leads up to the 50th day, when hopefully, we have readied ourselves to spiritually receive the Torah atop Mount Sinai on the festival of Shavuot.[81]

What is being counted, and why?

On Tu B'Shevat, we learned that wheat is one of the Seven Species of biblical plants revered in Israel. It is also Torah's springtime second crop that we are observing as we count its growing days. Imagine how much was riding on our ancestor's wheat crop, with no backup of grocery stores or online shopping.

Every evening during Sefirat HaOmer, we make a blessing, count the day, and say a special after-blessing. Our ancestors prayed for a successful harvest longing to fulfill the mitzvah of the 50th day, their Shavuot offering.[82] Since the destruction of the temple, this ritual has taken on a strictly spiritual meaning, as there is no temple to bring our offerings to—or is there? We know there is no outer temple, but the inner temple where the Divine dwells within each of us is always present and ready to receive our offerings. This is the holy focus of this time.

There is a custom to read one chapter a week of Pirkei Avot (Chapters of Our Fathers; usually translated as Ethics of our Fathers) between Pesach and Shavuot.[83] Many continue this practice until Rosh HaShanah, as the verses are full of our core ethical teachings. Immersing ourselves in them is ideal preparation for Shavuot and later for the new year.

These 49 days give us a chance to look within as they mirror our ancestors' 49-day journey from slavery to freedom, as they traveled from Egypt to Sinai. After 400 years of slavery, even though they had achieved physical freedom, the Israelites needed to learn how to become a free people. What better way than to emulate the One we were made in the image of as Genesis teaches, we are all created B'tzelem Elohim, in the image of God.[84]

We are getting to the heart of the matter when we investigate the Kabbalah of Sefirat HaOmer. There are 10 different attributes in which God manifests God's self to us and they are called the 10 *sefirot*. They are divided into two categories: the three intellectual sefirot of *chochma* (wisdom), *bina* (understanding), and *daat* (knowledge), an acronym for ChaBad; and the seven emotional attributes

---

80 Leviticus 23:15–16
81 Leviticus 23:15
82 Leviticus 23:17
83 Mishna, Tractate Nizikin
84 Genesis 1:22, 26–27

of *chesed* (kindness), *gevurah* (strength), *tiferet* (beauty), *netzach* (victory), *hod* (splendor), *yesod* (foundation), and *malchut* (kingship). During these 49 days, we focus on the lower seven, one attribute per week, and each day we combine it with another of the seven attributes, making 49 unique combinations in all. What an exquisite example of how our tradition gifts us with so many entry ways to spark our inspiration as we work to refine and elevate ourselves.

What is so special about Lag B'Omer?

The Talmud relates a story about the famous and beloved Rabbi Akiva, who was known for his teachings being rooted in the Torah's "Love your neighbor as yourself."[85] It is said that between Passover and Shavuot, a horrific tragedy occurred whereby 24,000 of Rabbi Akiva's students died of a plague because they had not treated one another respectfully.[86] Midrash tells us that the plague ceased on Lag B'Omer. We are grateful the tragedy ended and infuse this day with the love and kindness taught by Rabbi Akiva.

One of the unique characteristics of the seven weeks is that it is a semi-mourning period during which we mourn the death of Rabbi Akiva's beloved students. There are varying opinions about how this is interpreted, but many people following mourning customs do not get married, get haircuts, or listen to music until Lag B'Omer, when all restrictions are lifted. Some, however, return to the mourning observances the next day and continue through the 49th day. Consult with your rabbi if you have a decision to make during the Counting of the Omer.

Rabbi Shimon bar Yochai, known by the acronym Rashbi, was Rabbi Akiva's greatest student and fortunately outlived the plague. He spent his lifetime disseminating Kabbalah teachings, which previously had been taught in secret to a select few and passed down from teacher to student. He is credited with having written the Zohar, the preeminent writings on Kabbalah, which made this private study available to the world. There is more than one story about our many traditions, but my favorite regarding why bows and arrows are associated with this day is as follows: To study and teach Torah, even when being pursued by the Romans, Rashbi would bring his students into the woods and bring along bows and arrows. This way, when the soldiers came upon them, they could pretend they were hunting. The great bonfires that are lit represent the sparks of Divine light that the study of Kabbalah brings forth. It is said that he told his students that the day of his death would be a day of his joy, so they should celebrate. The Kabbalists taught that when a

---

85   Leviticus 19:18
86   Talmud, Yevamot 62b

great teacher dies, the synthesis of all their teachings and good deeds come together in what I imagine to be like cosmic fireworks radiating out into the world. Although we do not celebrate other rabbis' yahrzeits with festivities, it is a tradition to do so for the Rashbi. This sage, who died over 18 centuries ago, draws thousands each year to his birthplace of Meron in Israel.

I have loved Sefirat HaOmer for a very long time and find counting the Omer and its daily meditations to be tremendously centering, uplifting, and inspiring. It took me longer to find the meaning and joy in Lag B'Omer, but it came to me at last.

In the same way that the Rashbi spoke to his students about his eventual death, my mother spoke to me my entire life about her death, of her tremendous gratitude and all the gifts she had received; and because she was grateful and happy, she wanted me, too, to be happy for the life she'd lived and not be imbued by sadness. I recall having many of these conversations as a child while being driven back from grocery shopping, or after swimming on a warm summer's day. I remember the time my mom spoke of this after visiting her mom, Grandma Ida, in the nursing home. For years, she visited her mother every day, despite Grandma's never showing a sign of recognition as my mom lovingly cared for her. These talks seemed to come out of nowhere, but were never that surprising nonetheless and were somehow comforting, as they were most certainly intended to be. They continued until the last day of my mother's life, when she once again instructed me not to be sad when she died. She told me to have a celebration because she had had a life she was profoundly grateful for. She had known love with my father that filled the depths of her soul. She told me she wasn't afraid to die and that my father, who had passed many years earlier, was just waiting for her to dance into his arms.

I never understood how she could expect me to be happy, or to celebrate. However, my brothers and I all did as she requested, including going out for dinner, which was at terrible odds with everything I knew and had studied about, everything I taught others about what to do when death occurs. Nowhere in the many Jewish books had I read was there anything about going out and celebrating when your mother dies. It is only now, over two decades since her passing, that I see just how Jewish her outlook was. Now I see that, like the Rashbi, she was just spreading her love, love whose sparks keep radiating out like one of those great oversize Lag B'Omer bonfires.

May we all be blessed to find our holy sparks. May we be on the lookout for them coming from any direction, sometimes from the most unexpected of places.

From the Cook

Lag B'Omer is another one of the holidays that was unknown to me. Zoe's explanation of the seven-week time of counting days between Passover and Shavuot brings meaning, and an aha moment when something connects, and more of an understanding of a subject is achieved.

Honestly, there are a few things that I learned on my own about Lag B'Omer: there are apps for your phone that will give you prompts to help you count the days, and that carob is one of the foods that has a relationship to the holiday. I also discovered that part of Lag B'Omer celebrations includes a bonfire. The open flames give inspiration to the kind of food that is cooked during the holiday—kebabs: beef kebabs, chicken kebabs, and vegetable kebabs. My friend Yaniv, who grew up in Israel, told me that when he was young he loved to add potatoes to the bonfire and cook them until their skins turned as black as coal and the insides were creamy, soft, and delicious.

For my recipes, I've focused, as usual, on the arrival of seasonal crops. Zoe mentioned barley as an honored springtime grain. I've included a barley recipe (page 126) in Chapter 8 that celebrates Tu B'Shevat, a holiday that recognizes the Seven Species of food mentioned in the Bible.

Risotto *with Fava Beans, Mint, Parsley, and Pecorino*

SERVES 4 TO 6

1 teaspoon baking soda

1¼ pounds fresh fava beans

8 cups vegetable stock or water

1 cup dry white vermouth

1 tablespoon neutral oil, such as canola or grapeseed

1 cup chopped yellow onion (about 1 small to medium onion)

1½ cups risotto-friendly rice: Vialone Nano (my favorite), Canaroli, Arborio

1 cup chopped fresh chives

½ cup chopped fresh mint, plus whole leaves for garnish

4 teaspoons unsalted butter

2 tablespoons grated Parmigiano

1 tablespoon olive oil

½ cup shaved Pecorino Romano

I can't help but think of springtime as *primavera*, the Italian word for the season that means "the first green." This risotto is inspired by the vegetable risottos created by the Jews of Venice so as to stay within kosher dietary law. Although they may have used goose fat to sauté the onions that start a risotto, I chose a neutral oil instead. And butter, to *mantecare* (finish) the risotto. Either way, this dish shouldn't be served with meat in any other part of your meal. A simple choice when a dish is as mouthwatering as this one.

1. Place a medium saucepan filled with water and the baking soda (to ensure that the beans keep their bright green color) over medium-high heat and bring to a boil. Remove the beans from their pods but leave the waxy membranes on the beans. Blanch for 2 to 3 minutes. Use a wire-mesh strainer to remove the beans from the pot.

2. Remove and discard the membranes and set the beans aside.

3. Combine the vegetable stock or water and the vermouth in a large saucepan and bring to a simmer.

4. Place a large heavy-bottomed skillet over medium heat on a burner near the simmering stock mixture. Heat the neutral oil in the skillet and sauté the onion until translucent—try to avoid browning it. Add the rice to the skillet and stir to coat with the oil. Add two ladlesful of the stock mixture and stir continuously until the rice has absorbed the liquid. Keep adding the two ladlesful at a time until the rice is tender. Add the chives, mint, butter, and Parmigiano. Stir to combine.

5. Immediately add the olive oil to a small skillet over medium heat. Add the fava beans and toss in the oil until hot.

6. To serve: Top the risotto with the fava beans. Cover them with shards of shaved Pecorino.

Charlotte's Beet and Strawberry Borscht

MAKES 6 TO 7 CUPS

2 quarts water

1 teaspoon salt, plus more to taste as desired

1½ pounds beets, leaf and root ends removed, scrubbed clean

1 to 2 teaspoons rapadura sugar, Sucanat, or light brown sugar

1 quart strawberries, hulled and rinsed

1 tablespoon good-quality balsamic vinegar

Optional garnishes: sour cream, Greek-style yogurt, mascarpone, mint leaves

Although rapadura sugar is brown, it's not the same ingredient as brown sugar. Brown sugar is refined white sugar with molasses added back into it. You might find rapadura sugar by another name, Sucanat. It's made by juicing sugar cane, then filtering the juice, drying it, and then grinding it into tiny granules. I love the way rapadura sugar sweetens fresh fruit, becoming part of it.

My friend and agent Charlotte developed this recipe a few years ago. I first tasted it at her home and was immediately smitten. It's one of those recipes that depends on the quality of its ingredients, which are basically two—beets and strawberries. The earthy, minerally, tart, and sweet combination of components elevates this borscht to a sweet-and-sour soup to something you may never have tasted but fall headlong in love with at first spoonful. If real love were only that easy. Charlotte, as do I, now waits with anticipation for the arrival of local strawberries to give the soup just the right zing. The addition of a thick, milky garnish, swirled through the borscht, turns it into a color that no doubt has inspired many couturiers: shocking pink. I once served it topped with unsweetened whipped cream and chopped salted pistachios.

1. Combine the water and salt in a large, nonreactive pot. Cut the beets, skin on, into quarters or sixths, depending on their size, and add to the pot. Bring to a boil. Lower the heat to a simmer, add the sugar, and cook until a tester easily passes through the beets, 1 to 1½ hours.

2. Meanwhile, place the hulled strawberries in a bowl with the vinegar and toss to combine.

3. When the beets are cooked through, remove from the heat and let cool until just warm. Use an immersion blender to process the beets in their cooking water until they resemble oatmeal.

4. Add the macerated strawberries to the beets. Use an immersion blender to incorporate the strawberries.

5. Serve at room temperature, or chilled with your choice of garnish.

6. The borscht will keep, refrigerated, for several days. It can be frozen for up to a month.

Rhubarb and Caramelized Onion Schiacciata

MAKES 4 SCHIACCIATA; SERVES 10 TO 12, OR MORE AS A COCKTAIL SNACK

SCHIACCIATA DOUGH

1 packet (2¼ teaspoons) active dry yeast

1 teaspoon sugar

1 cup warm water, about 90°F

3 cups all-purpose flour, plus more for dusting

2 teaspoons salt

⅓ cup extra-virgin olive oil, plus more for rising

TOPPING

2 tablespoons olive oil

About 6 red rhubarb stalks, cut on the bias into 1-inch pieces (about 3 cups sliced)

2 medium white onions, sliced thinly (3 cups sliced)

4 teaspoons honey

½ teaspoon salt

¼ teaspoon Aleppo pepper flakes or freshly ground black pepper

1 tablespoon pomegranate molasses

4 ounces crumbled feta

2 teaspoons chopped fresh rosemary leaves

In my ongoing quest to find more things to make with rhubarb (which I love)—especially savory dishes—I landed on this one. Rosemary is its natural companion, making it just the right topping for this *schiacciata* (crushed or smashed) flatbread. Cut it into narrow pieces to serve as a cocktail snack; or into wider ones to serve with a salad.

1. Make the dough: Combine the yeast, sugar, and warm water in a 2-cup measuring cup. Let stand in a draft-free area until foamy, about 15 minutes. Combine the flour and salt in a large bowl. Stir the olive oil into the yeast mixture, then add the yeast mixture to the flour. Mix well. Turn out onto a floured surface. Knead until soft and elastic, 3 to 4 minutes.

2. Swish a few tablespoons of olive oil in a large bowl and place the dough in it. Cover and place in a warm, draft-free environment to rise. It should double in size in 45 minutes to an hour. Punch down. Cut into four pieces and return to the bowl. Re-cover.

3. Prepare the topping: Heat the olive oil in a medium skillet over medium heat. Add the rhubarb, onions, honey, pepper, and salt. Toss to combine. Cook just long enough to soften the vegetables, 3 to 4 minutes. Remove from the heat. Let cool, then stir in the pomegranate molasses.

4. Heat the oven to 450°F. Have ready two half baking sheets or jelly-roll pans.

5. Stretch each piece of dough into a log that measures about 3 by 12 inches. Pat down in place on the pans, two logs per pan.

6. Divide the rhubarb mixture into four equal portions and spread thinly over the dough. Distribute the feta over each schiacciata. Sprinkle the rosemary over the feta. Bake until the crust is golden and the feta has melted, about 15 minutes.

7. Serve hot from the oven or at room temperature. Cut into 1- to 2-inch pieces to serve.

Rhubarb is grown in many of the communities of the Jewish Diaspora—Russia, Turkey, Iran, and Greece—where it's mostly used in savory applications. Fortunately for us cooks, this plant, with its astringent, almost citrus flavor, straddles the seasons when Passover, Lag B'Omer, and Shavuot are celebrated. Be sure to use only the stalks; rhubarb leaves and any blossoms are toxic.

Sugar Snap Peas *with Anchovy Sauce, Toasted Pine Nuts, and Preserved Lemons*

SERVES 4 TO 5

1 quart fresh sugar snap peas

1 teaspoon baking soda

2 tablespoons olive oil

2 tablespoons pine nuts

5 anchovy fillets (packed in olive oil)

½ teaspoon Aleppo pepper flakes or freshly ground black pepper

1 teaspoon freshly grated orange zest (from 1 large orange)

2 tablespoons freshly grated Parmesan

4 teaspoons tiny-diced Preserved Lemons (page 41)

I think of this dish as a kind of sugar snap pea Caesar salad—without the egg. Look for freshly harvested sugar snaps. The older they get, the tougher they become, and older peas can reach pebblelike consistency.

1. Pull the strings off the peas: Start at the vine end and unzip them by pulling down the length of the pod. Sometimes, if you're lucky, you can remove both sides of the strings in one go.

2. Place a medium pot of water and the baking soda over medium-high heat. Blanch the sugar snaps for 3 minutes. Transfer to a paper towel–lined tray in a single layer to cool down.

3. Heat the olive oil in a medium skillet over medium heat. When it's hot, add the pine nuts and let toast until just golden, taking care not to burn them; they will burn if not carefully watched. Lower the heat a bit and immediately add the anchovy fillets to the pine nuts. Use a wooden spoon to squash the anchovies, helping them melt into the oil. Add the pepper and orange zest.

4. Transfer the cool sugar snaps to a medium bowl. Pour the sauce over them and stir to coat all the peas.

5. To serve: Place the dressed peas on a serving platter. Sprinkle the Parmesan over the top. Then, sprinkle the diced preserved lemons over all.

Roasted Rhubarb and Orange Dairy-Free Custard

SERVES 4 TO 6

1 teaspoon fragrant and nutty oil, such as walnut or macadamia

1 pound red rhubarb stalks, cut on the bias into 1-inch pieces

1 cup sugar

4 large eggs

1½ cups oat milk

1 cup coconut yogurt

1 teaspoon orange blossom water

Zest of 1 large orange (about 1 teaspoon)

1 orange, peeled, pith and pits removed, cut into ¼-inch slices

Like the Lemon-Limoncello Olive Oil Cake (page 152) in the Purim chapter, this recipe was developed to serve to my lactose-intolerant friends. These days, finding substitutes for cow-produced milk is easy. There are so many available plant-based milks it's worth experimenting with recipes to avoid the discomfort that often comes with over-consumption of dairy products.

1. Heat the oven to 350ºF.

2. Oil a 9-inch gratin dish with the oil. Place the cut rhubarb in the dish and cover with the sugar. Toss to combine. Bake until the rhubarb collapses and begins to caramelize, about 30 minutes. Remove the dish from the oven. Leave the oven on.

3. Whisk together the eggs, oat milk, yogurt, orange blossom water, and orange zest in a medium bowl. Pour the mixture over the rhubarb. Cut the orange slices in half. Place on top of the custard in a decorative way.

4. Bake until the custard is firm, 30 to 40 minutes.

5. Serve warm or at room temperature.

Carob Bonbons

MAKES THIRTY TO THIRTY-FIVE 1-INCH ROUND BONBONS

One 12-ounce bag unsweetened carob chips

1 cup wheat germ, plus more for rolling

1 cup chunky peanut butter

You may have guessed that dogs play a big role in my life. I've had series of long-lived mutts that have come off the streets of New York City, and my latest, who came off the streets of Los Angeles. I think these creatures deserve something extra special at holiday time, just as we do. Unlike chocolate (which is toxic to dogs and cats), carob is pet-friendly. I found a recipe something like this one in a recipe book for dogs. It's Bean (my little terrier mutt) approved.

1. Place the carob chips in the top of a large double boiler over medium heat and stir continually until they melt. Remove from the heat.

2. Add the wheat germ and peanut butter. Stir until the mixture thickens enough to form a ball. You may have to let the mixture cool, which you can accomplish by refrigerating it for a few minutes.

3. I use a melon baller to make 1-inch balls. Or form them by rolling a heaping tablespoon of the mixture in the palm of your hands.

4. Place the balls on a wheat germ–covered plate. Roll them in the wheat germ to cover.

5. Store the bonbons, refrigerated, in an airtight container.

6. Give them to your dog only as a special treat. You may like them as well.

Zoe told us that one of the protagonists of Lag B'Omer was Rabbi Shimon bar Yochai, known as Rashbi, who brought his son, Rabbi Elazar, into the woods to escape their Roman oppressors. While in the woods, they stayed strong from consuming a subsistence diet of carobs from a tree that, miraculously, grew at the entrance to their hideout, a cave. The carob tree produces long, shiny, dark brown pods filled with seeds and pulp that have a sweet and toasty flavor. Carob is often used in its own gelatinous form, or powdered for cooking and baking, or as a stand-in for those with an intolerance to chocolate.

Strawberry-Rhubarb Sauce

MAKES ABOUT 1½ PINTS

4 cups hulled and sliced
strawberries

4 cups sliced red rhubarb
stalks

¾ cup sugar

½ cup freshly squeezed
orange juice

½ cup Campari

Consider this recipe a lagniappe to the chapter. It takes advantage of the magical moment in the season when the rhubarb harvest crosses into the strawberry harvest to create a sauce worthy of many applications: to make a sorbet, as a companion to Masa Tiganitas (page 164), or pressed through a sieve and added to an icy glass of Prosecco to make a cocktail. The addition of Campari—which has rhubarb as one of its ingredients—to the sauce flirts with the rhubarb to give the sauce its mysterious flavor.

1. Combine the strawberries, rhubarb, sugar, orange juice, and Campari in a large, nonreactive saucepan.

2. Cook over medium heat until the ingredients collapse and the sauce clings to the spoon like syrup.

3. Remove from the heat. Let cool. Refrigerate in glass jars, or process in canning jars according to the manufacturer's directions.

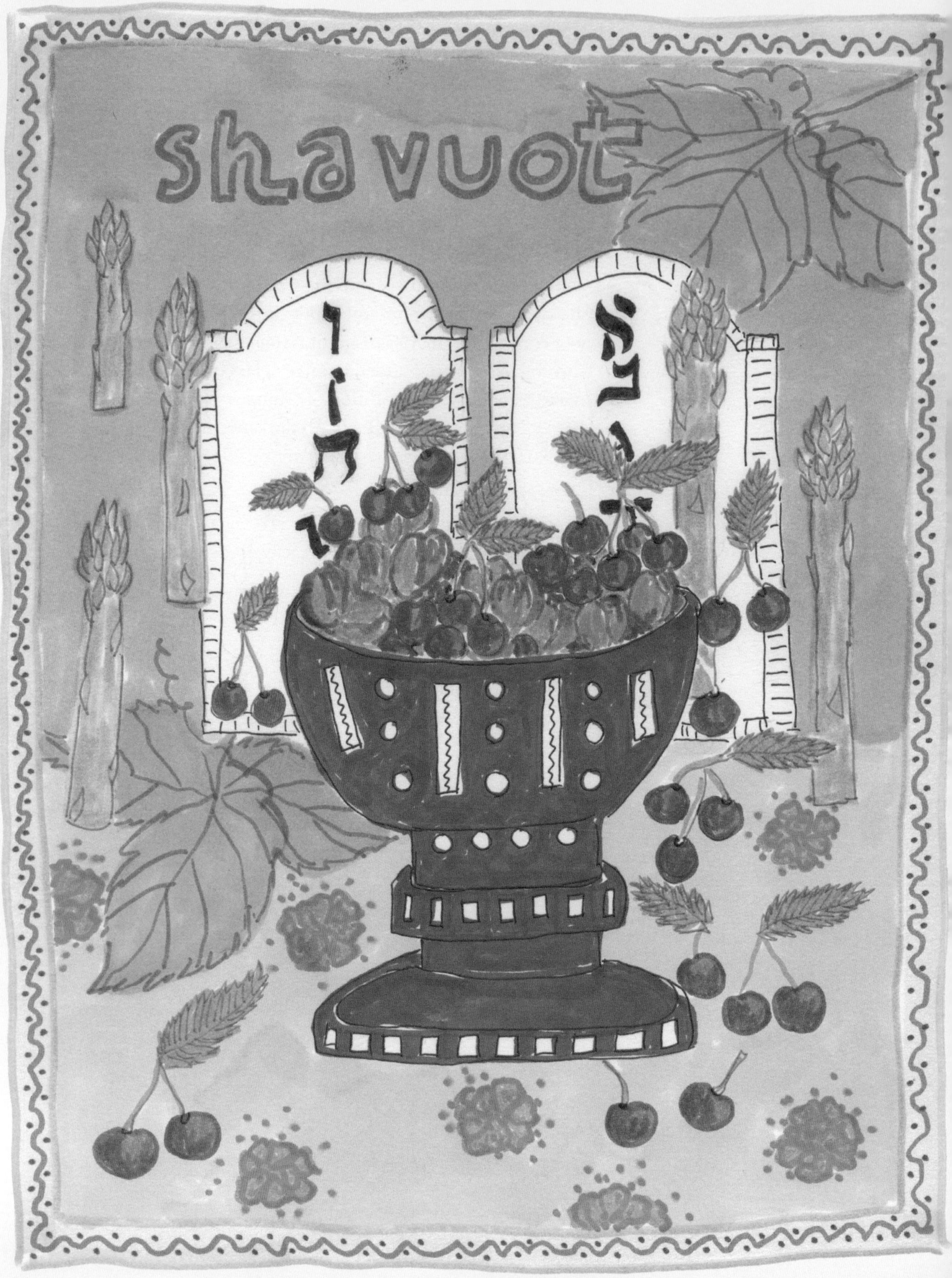
shavuot

CHAPTER TWELVE

Shavuot

*Just six days into her first quarter,
a celebration is called for
announcing God's giving
and our receiving
the gift of Torah!*

From the Rabbi

Susan: *Does this holiday begin at the end of counting the Omer?*
What exactly is being celebrated?

Zoe: All our holidays can and do stand alone, but they are more potent when connected with one another. They are much like a family of diverse personalities that requires every name to complete the family tree. The remarkable thing about Shavuot's date is that it can't exist without the festival of Passover. They are in fact a team—what one begins, the other completes. As was outlined in our last chapter, we have seven reflective weeks, Sefirat HaOmer, to prepare for this holiday. In Hebrew, *shavuot* means "weeks." On Passover, the Israelites started their journey as slaves in Egypt and headed out as freed people toward the Promised Land. Seven weeks later, God called Moses to ascend Mount Sinai to receive the Torah on behalf of all the people.[87] Torah gives this special designation of "festival" to Shavuot, along with Sukkot and Pesach. The fuller our experience of one, the more meaningful it has the potential to make the next.

In one of your talks, I heard you say that the priest brought two loaves
of bread to the temple on Shavuot. What is the significance of this?

Different types of offerings were made during temple days. The people made long pilgrimages to Jerusalem and each family brought the first fruits from their

---

87   Exodus 20:2–17, Deuteronomy 5:6–21

crops of the Seven Species, the same ones described in Chapter 8, on Tu B'Shevat: the grains and fruits designated by Torah representing the abundance of the land: wheat, barley, grapes, figs, pomegranates, olives, and dates. The Kohanim (priests) brought two loaves of bread made from the newly harvested wheat. They also brought burnt animal sacrifices, grain offerings, and libations. Although many people long to rebuild the temple in Jerusalem and return to rituals that were performed when it stood, I am deeply grateful that we no longer sacrifice animals and pray we never do so again. Unlike the fruits or even animals that were offered whole and in their natural state, the loaves are really in their own category. They were made from the wheat that was a gift from God along with the help of humans who took care of the crop, harvested the wheat, made the flour, mixed it with wet ingredients, kneaded the dough, made a fire, and baked it. The breads, a symbol of our partnership with the Divine, are a perfect example of how we rely on God and on how God counts on us. Our tradition teaches us that we are here to bring the spiritual into the physical realm. Making bread is a marvelous fulfillment of this. It invites us to be present and centered in gratitude and wonder. It truly is a miracle every time we eat food. Saying a *bracha* (blessing) before we eat elevates the moment, and brings us full circle.

What does it mean that we were all there on Mount Sinai when the Ten Commandments were given?

In Torah, Shavuot is described as an agricultural festival. It was over time that the rabbis formed their understanding that this festival was Zeman Matan Torateinu (The Time of the Giving of Our Torah). Its name reflects an action occurring in the present tense. Not only were the Aseret HaDebrot (Ten Sayings, or Ten Commandments) given, but we are taught that the entire Torah was given. This refers to the entire written Torah and the Oral Torah, the Mishnah. Our tradition encourages us to ask questions and so we must ask, What does this mean and how is this even conceivable? We are instructed in Judaism to ask questions to explore and unlock the meaning encoded within Torah. Receiving the answer isn't guaranteed, but the process is a reward in and of itself.

Toward the end of Moses's life, he gave an eloquent speech to the Israelites who were gathered around him saying, "Not only with you do I make this covenant and this oath, but with those who are standing here with us today before Adonai our God, and with those who are not with us here today."[88]

This to me, is one of the most stunning phrases in all of Torah. It demonstrates how during this festival, time is erased, as past and present become one. Midrash

---

88 Deuteronomy 29:13–14

tells us that when the Torah was given, every plant in the desert bloomed. We, too, pray for all our dry places to open and birth resplendent gardens.

Shavuot symbolizes a marriage between the Divine and the Jewish people. The gift was given and received, and in that exchange, a *brit* (covenant) was formed.

At our synagogue I like to put up a chuppah, a wedding canopy, on Shavuot and invite people to hold the Torah as they stand under the tallit (prayer shawl) covering. It brings me to tears feeling the palpable emotion as each person receives the Torah. In this way, we are brought to Mount Sinai.

How is Ruth connected to Shavuot?

We read the biblical Book of Ruth on Shavuot and it carries within it a profoundly powerful message. Naomi, a poor woman from a harsh community, suffered beyond tragic loss with the death of her husband, and shortly thereafter, her two sons. The story might have ended there, but because of her phenomenal resilience, she went forward in her life and impacted the world.

Naomi's daughters-in-law, Orpah and Ruth, were both Moabites. After their husbands died, she told them to return to their families and begin their lives anew. Ruth responded with the famous words, "Do not urge me to leave you or to turn back from you. For wherever you go, I will go, and wherever you lodge, I will lodge, your people will be my people, and your God, my God."[89]

I love that this declaration of love and devotion is offered from a young woman to her mother-in-law. It is truly one of my favorite passages in all of Tanach. Ruth is cherished and looked after and finds love during the barley harvest with a man named Boaz. He treats her with respect and dignity, marries her, and together they have a baby. In the lineage that follows, King David descended from Ruth, the Moabite widow who was mightily blessed. Reading the Book of Ruth, we see all the ways this book addresses social justice, love, death, trauma, and rebirth. It is the perfect companion for a festival about harvest and finding inner meaning and purpose.

How would you sum up Shavuot for the uninformed, like I am?

One of the most famous Talmudic stories captures the essence of Torah, which is at the heart of Shavuot. It involves a man who wanted to convert to Judaism and his encounter with two different Talmudic sages, Hillel and Shammai. Their different approaches to learning and interpreting Torah is well documented in the Talmud. The man went to Shammai saying that he would convert to Judaism

---

89   Ruth 1:16

189

if Shammai could teach him the entirety of Torah while he stood on one foot.[90] The teacher was so furious that he pushed him out the door, but the man was not deterred. He went to Hillel with the same demand and Hillel converted him. Afterward, he told him; "That which is hateful to you, do not do to another. That is the entire Torah; the rest is commentary. Go study."

This is the central idea of Torah and Judaism. It is alive and ever growing. It is looking for Torah within and determining what to do and what not to do. We look for Torah within ourselves and remember that all of us are created in the image of the Divine. Wherever I go, I am searching for those Divine sparks.

As I now love to say on Shavuot, *B'ezrat HaShem* (with Hashem's help), see you on Mount Sinai.

Shavuot, unlike our other holidays, does not have its own date. Torah tells us to count 50 days from the second day of Passover to arrive at the date for this festival.[91]

91   Leviticus 23:15–16

When a holiday has more than one name, like a person with nicknames, they each reflect a unique aspect of the special time. In the Torah, Shavuot is referred to as Chag HaKatzir (Harvest Festival)[92] and Chag HaBikurim (Festival of the First Fruits).[93] In the Talmud, it is named Zeman Matan Torateinu (The Time of the Giving of Our Torah). Our tradition took this holiday from an agricultural one and transformed it into celebrating the greatest moment in the history of our people.

92   Exodus 34:22
93   Exodus 34:22

---

90   Shabbat 31a

From the Cook

For me Shavuot is an opportunity to use more of the springtime harvest, and a little coming attraction of the luscious summertime crop with the early-ish appearance of apricots and sour cherries. And, of course, blintzes. Any excuse for blintzes.

Sephardic Jews make a cake called *siete cielos* (seven heavens) to represent Mount Sinai. Syrian Jews make a cheese-stuffed pancake called *ataiyef*, not necessarily specific to Shavuot but often served on the holiday.

Salade Russe

SERVES 6

SALAD

½ pound beets, unpeeled, root and leaf ends removed

1½ pounds waxy potatoes, peeled and cut into ½-inch dice

¾ pound carrots, peeled and cut into ½-inch dice

1 cup thawed petit pois

MAYONNAISE

1 large egg

2 tablespoons freshly squeezed lemon juice

½ teaspoon salt

¾ cup olive oil

¼ cup canola oil

TO SERVE

4 hard-boiled large eggs

8 to 10 cornichons or gherkins, cut into fans (see Note)

1 heaping tablespoon capers

This salad has been a popular side to eggs, roasted meats, and fish since it was created by chef Lucian Olivier in the mid-19th century for the Moscow restaurant Hermitage, and was subsequently popular all over Russia—and now needs a new name to retain its favor. Why not call it what it is: potato and beet salad. The salad, with the addition of *petit pois*—frozen, of course, carrots, and fanciful garnishes, is just what you want to serve for any holiday. Especially Shavuot, a quintessential harvest holiday.

MAKE THE SALAD

1. Heat the oven to 300°F.

2. Wrap the beets in parchment paper. Place on a baking sheet and bake until a tester easily passes through them, 45 minutes.

3. Steam the potatoes 8 to 10 minutes. Remove from the steamer and place on a tray in a single layer to cool.

4. Steam the carrots 8 to 10 minutes, remove from the steamer and place on a tray in a single layer to cool.

5. Blanch the peas for 2 minutes in a saucepan of boiling water and transfer to layers of paper towels to drain.

6. Once the beets are cooked, remove them from the parchment. Let cool. Peel them and cut into ½-inch dice.

MAKE THE MAYONNAISE

1. Combine the egg, lemon juice, and salt in a food processor or blender. Run the machine until the egg is pale and foamy. Slowly add the oils until a stiff mayonnaise is achieved.

NOTE: *To make cornichon fans: Thinly slice the pickle from one end toward the vine end, stopping just before it reaches the opposite end. You should be able to make three or four slices. Fan out the pickle when ready to use.*

TO SERVE

1. Combine the beets, potatoes, carrots, and peas in a bowl. Start by adding half of the mayonnaise and mix until fully incorporated into the vegetables. Add more mayonnaise as desired, but keep some to coat the presentation.

2. Create a dome with the salad by packing it into a bowl, then turning it upside down onto a serving platter. "Frost" the dome with a thin film of the leftover mayonnaise. Decorate the dome with three sliced hard-boiled eggs as a border around the bottom edge. Place the cornichon fans in another row around the dome. Sprinkle the capers over the top. Cut the fourth egg into thin wedges to make a flowerlike decoration at the top of the dome.

Grilled Goat Cheese–Stuffed Vine Leaves

Grapes are one of the Seven Species mentioned in the Bible. Here's example of how populations, where grapes grow, use the fruits' leaves as a natural wrapper for a filling. You may be accustomed to the Greek-style vine leaves stuffed with rice and lots of dill. Give this one a try. Smear it, piping hot off the grill, on a piece of toasted bread.

MAKES 16 TO 18 STUFFED VINE LEAVES

16 to 18 vine leaves

8 ounces soft goat cheese

1 heaping tablespoon chopped fresh flat-leaf parsley

1 heaping tablespoon chopped fresh chives

2 teaspoons tiny-diced Preserved Lemons (page 41)

1 tablespoon toasted pine nuts

1 heaping tablespoon capers, rinsed

⅛ to ¼ teaspoon Aleppo pepper flakes

2 tablespoons olive oil

1. Rinse the vine leaves in cold running water. Drape the rinsed leaves around the edge of a bowl to drain. They can be piled on one another. Or place them on a dinner plate or a tray to drain.

2. Make the filling: Combine the cheese, parsley, chives, preserved lemons, pine nuts, capers, and pepper flakes in a bowl. Thoroughly combine the ingredients.

3. Heat an outdoor grill. (Alternatively, heat a grill pan or cast-iron pan over high heat after you complete step 4.)

4. To fill: Work with three or four leaves at a time. Place them flat on a plate or work surface, vein side up, stem end facing you, and put a rounded tablespoon of the cheese mixture in the middle of the leaf near the stem. Fold the stem end over the cheese, then fold both sides over the middle. Roll up into a cigar. Repeat to fill the other leaves.

5. Smear the olive oil over each bundle. Place, seam side up, on the hot grill for 2 to 3 minutes. Flip and grill another 2 to 3 minutes until leaves are deeply bronzed and appear crispy. Remove from the heat.

6. Serve immediately with toasted bread.

Asparagus *with Rose Harissa Mayonnaise and Preserved Lemon Bread Crumbs*

SERVES 4

1¼ pounds asparagus, peeled
  if the spears are thick
  or the harvest date is
  unknown; woody ends cut
  off and discarded

1 large egg

1 tablespoon juice from
  Preserved Lemons
  (page 41)

¼ to ½ teaspoon rose harissa
  (more if you like extra
  spicy)

1 cup olive oil

2 tablespoons tiny-diced
  Preserved Lemons
  (page 41)

⅓ cup panko bread crumbs

Salt (for me, not necessary
  as the preserved lemons
  transport lots of salt)

Rose harissa has become one of my favorite ingredients. I'm attracted to the way its combination of ingredients—peppers (hot and mild); such spices as cumin, caraway, and coriander; and garlic and rose petals or rose water—adds depth and a kind of subtle fire to other elements of a dish, without scorching your tongue. It's the roses that calm it. Harissa is an oft-used ingredient in North African and Middle Eastern cuisine, either in paste form (olive oil is added) or powdered.

I'm not a big fan of plunging cooked asparagus into icy water. I prefer to pull out the asparagus when it's a bit undercooked and let it finish cooking on its own as it cools. It's less water-logged that way.

1. Place a large, deep skillet (so the asparagus can lie down) of salted water over high heat and bring to a boil. Lower the heat to medium and add the asparagus. Cook for 5 to 8 minutes. Transfer to a paper towel-lined tray to cool.

2. Make the mayonnaise: Combine the egg, preserved lemon juice, and rose harissa in a blender or food processor. Run the machine until the egg turns pale yellow. Continuing to run the machine, slowly add enough olive oil—about ¾ cup—to form a pourable, not thick, mayonnaise. Transfer to a bowl and set aside.

3. Heat the remaining olive oil in a medium skillet over medium-high heat. Add the panko to the hot oil and toast until the crumbs are golden, about 90 seconds. Remove from the heat and stir in the diced preserved lemons.

4. Arrange the asparagus either on a serving platter or individual plates, bud ends all in the same direction. Pour the mayonnaise over the top half of the spears and sprinkle the panko over it. Serve right away.

Cannoli Blintzes *with Amarene*

SERVES 10, PERHAPS WITH SOME LEFTOVER FILLING TO USE ON TOAST

FILLING

1 pound whole-milk ricotta

¼ cup sour cream

1 large egg, beaten

¼ cup chopped amarene cotte (recipe follows)

¼ cup chopped pistachios

¼ cup chopped semisweet chocolate or small semisweet chocolate chips

BLINTZES

4 large eggs, beaten

¾ cup whole milk

¼ cup water

Pinch of salt

1 cup all-purpose flour

8 tablespoons (1 stick) unsalted butter for frying

The route to this recipe is one that I take every year during the sour cherry harvest, *amarene cotte*, and then repeat from time to time throughout the year with cherries that I've frozen in quart containers to use until the next sour cherry harvest arrives.

Other ingredients were then added to this Italian-style sour cherry preparation to create a bang-on filling for blintzes. Enjoy them for breakfast, brunch, or dessert.

MAKE THE FILLING

1. Place the ricotta, sour cream, and egg in a medium bowl. Add the chopped amarene cotte, pistachios, and chocolate to the bowl. Mix together thoroughly. Set aside.

MAKE THE BLINTZES

1. Combine the eggs, milk, water, salt, and flour in a blender. Blend until a smooth batter is achieved. Alternatively, place the ingredients in a bowl and whisk together. Let the batter rest for 30 to 45 minutes.

2. Place a 7- to 8-inch skillet over medium heat and add about 2 teaspoons of the butter. Pour ¼ cup of batter into the skillet and tilt it around so the batter covers the entire bottom. Don't let the blintz brown.

3. Flip the blintz over and cook for another 30 seconds. Transfer to a tray.

4. Repeat, adding more butter with each blintz, until the batter is finished. The blintzes can be stored, overlapping, on the tray.

5. Assemble the blintzes: Line them up, two or three at a time, and place 2 tablespoons of the filling in a line along the area of the blintz closest to you, leaving space on the bottom and sides for folding.

6. Fold the bottom up toward the filling, then fold the sides over the middle. Roll up.

7. Add more butter to the skillet that you used to make the blintzes. Fry two at a time, seam side down, until golden, then flip and fry the other side until golden. You may fry the sides as well until golden.

8. Serve topped with amarene cotte.

AMARENE COTTE

MAKES ABOUT 1 QUART

One 750 ml bottle red wine, not too full bodied, such as Valpolicella or Beaujolais

1½ cups sugar

1 cinnamon stick

1 teaspoon whole cloves

2 quarts sour cherries

1. Combine the wine, sugar, cinnamon stick, and cloves in a large, nonreactive pan over medium heat. Reduce by half, 30 to 35 minutes.

2. Meanwhile, pit the cherries. Remove the cinnamon and cloves from the reduced wine and add the cherries to the pan. Cook for 15 minutes more. Remove from the heat and let cool.

3. Use in the blintzes recipe. However, you'll have leftovers to top ice cream, a cheesecake, and so on.

4. The cherries may be stored in an airtight glass jar, refrigerated, for up to a month.

It's a curious thing—this obsession with cheesecake, kugel, and blintzes on Shavuot. I searched for answers as to why. Shavuot as I understand it doesn't have a seder, or such symbols as shofars or eight-candle menorahs to define it. So, for popular appeal, the holiday became focused on sweet dairy desserts—perhaps as a reference to the Promised Land, the Land of Milk and Honey, Israel.

Apricot Butter

MAKES 2 CUPS

3¼ pounds apricots, halved and pitted

1¾ cups freshly squeezed orange juice

½ cup sugar

¼ cup freshly squeezed lemon juice

I love the orchard fruits that grow in my area of the Hudson Valley. Apricots may be my favorite harvest. However, their season is fleeting. What I don't eat right away, I make into apricot butter to freeze and pull out for special occasions. The most special occasion of all is to fill Hamantaschen (page 150).

1. Combine the apricots, orange juice, sugar, and lemon juice in a large, nonreactive saucepan. Bring to a boil. Simmer over high heat, stirring so the fruit doesn't stick to the bottom, until the apricots are tender, 10 to 15 minutes. Lower the heat to low and simmer, stirring, until thick, about an hour.

2. Use a silicone spatula to scrape the apricot butter from the pan into a food processor. Let cool. Then, puree until smooth.

3. Transfer the apricot butter to jars and refrigerate for up to a week. Or transfer to lidded plastic containers and freeze for up to a year. Or a combination: eat some now on buttered biscuits, and save some for hamantaschen.

CHAPTER THIRTEEN

Tisha B'Av

The moon in her first quarter,
graces us with light
to illuminate the darkness of an empty
Ark of the Covenant.

From the Rabbi

Susan: *Why is Tisha B'Av considered the darkest day in the Jewish calendar?*

Zoe: On this day, we recall tragedies in our history that occurred on or around Tisha B'Av, which translates as the ninth day of the Hebrew month of Av. Like Yom Kippur, it is a 25-hour fast day. We mourn for the Holy Temple that was destroyed not once but twice, the First Temple in 587 BCE by the Babylonians, and the Second Temple in 70 CE by the Romans. Among other devastating events that happened on Tisha B'Av, all the Jews were expelled from England in 1290, and from Spain in 1492.

Rabbis have even been able to calculate a pivotal loss described in the Book of Exodus that took place on this date. Moses was leading the Israelites, and in this part of the story, they were nearing the land promised to them by God, the one described as flowing with milk and honey. God instructed Moses to send 12 men, one from each of the tribes, to go and scout the land.[94] After 40 days of spying, they returned and 10 of the men gave terrifying reports of a country that devours its settlers and whose people are the size of giants.[95] Upon hearing this, fear and anxiety spread like wildfire throughout the community. Almost everyone lost all faith and didn't want to enter the land. Moses had to plead with the Almighty to forgive them for wanting to return to Egypt. Even though they

---

94   Numbers 13:1
95   Numbers 13:32–33

had been slaves there, they longed for what was familiar. They were forgiven, nevertheless made to wander for 40 years in the desert, one year for each of the days the spies had spent in the land. To add to their punishment, those who had bitterly complained would not receive the reward of entering the land after all, but would die while in the wilderness.

Tisha B'Av, however, is also reserved for the birth of Mashiach (the Messiah), and so you can see, our tradition predicts a silver lining, a light that will radiate beyond the darkness that, up until now, has overshadowed this date.

What exactly was the Temple?

Beit HaMikdash (literally, the Holy Home) was its name and it was certainly nothing like any of us has known. To even try to envision what our ancestors experienced requires suspending our modern-day notions of God, synagogue, and even spirituality. For us, the concept that God is everywhere is central to our modern-day Judaism. But for the ancients, the football field–size Temple was built as a holy dwelling-place for the Divine. Talmud teaches that within the Torah, there are 613 Mitzvot (mitzvahs),[96] and remarkably, two-thirds of them could only be fulfilled when the Temple stood. Even though our ancestors pilgrimaged there on special occasions, sacrifices and a myriad of rituals were offered daily. Violence erupting on this holy ground, not once, but twice, created fault lines that forever changed the landscape of our people's way of life and relationship to their Creator.

How can we imagine what it must have been like? It isn't like today, when we can go to this synagogue or that one, pick the one that prays with the melodies we like most, aligns with our preferred demonization, or where our friends attend, or even our children's friends go to Hebrew school. There was only one place to worship, and the importance of this holy place cannot be overstated. When it was destroyed, it was believed that God went into exile. Imagine not knowing where God was or where to find the Divine. The loss both times was devastating for the individual and for the community who like God was now exiled.

There is a buildup to its observance that begins three weeks earlier on the 17th of (the Hebrew month of) Tammuz, which in Hebrew is Shivah Asar B'Tammuz. On this date, we mournfully recall when the Roman army breached the walls of Jerusalem. After three weeks, nearly one million Jews had been killed before the troops reached and then razed the Temple. There are other tragedies that occurred on this day in our history, and once again the rabbis have been able to calculate that our ancestors turned away from God on this date.

---

96 Makkot 23b

In Exodus,[97] we read that Moses was called by God and ascended Mount Sinai for 40 days. After his ecstatic experience of receiving the Ten Commandments, while holding the tablets God had inscribed God's self, he descended the mountain and discovered the people worshiping the golden calf. Once again, our people had lost their faith and their way. The confluence of these events caused Moses to smash those precious tablets on this very day.

This is a minor fast day where we fast between dawn and nightfall. It is the beginning of the period we call The Three Weeks and continues until the end of Tisha B'Av. During these three weeks, we lessen our joy and don't have weddings, haircuts, or concerts, and follow other mourning rituals. There are varying customs, so please speak to your rabbi if you need guidance. It is important to note that if either of the two days falls on Shabbat, the day is postponed until Sunday so that Shabbat keeps her joy.

On Tisha B'Av, some synagogues follow the custom of removing the Torahs from the ark prior to the service. The first time I was preparing to lead services on this night, I removed the Torahs from the ark, placing them safely in the rabbi's study. When the ark was opened during the service, even though I knew it would be empty, it was utterly shocking and quite devastating to discover the void within.

I know that this isn't the only fasting day in the Jewish calendar—are they connected?

Why do we fast on Tisha B'Av? It isn't only food that we refrain from; there are other things we abstain from as well. But to me the most remarkable one is that we don't study Torah except for readings having to do with the destruction of the Temple and other related tragedies. We read Lamentations (Eichah), which prophecies the destruction of the First Temple and the exile of the Israelites. It isn't that we are torturing ourselves by fasting, and by the way, there are of course exceptions as to who should not fast, but what this is really about is refraining from what gives us joy. It is much like removing a drop of wine from our cup as we recall each of the plagues on Passover. We are not trying to make ourselves miserable; rather, we are giving ourselves space to allow ourselves to really dip down in to these horrific memories of our people. It is time to look within.

The Talmud teaches, "One who mourns Jerusalem will merit to see her happiness."[98] Equally important to remembering the past is to build a bridge to the future, so we turn ourselves and pray for the rebuilding and healing of all that

---

97 Exodus 32:1–4
98 Taanit 30b

is broken and torn down. We recommit ourselves to Tikkun Olam (the repairing of the world), to do our part in making it whole. Perhaps this is how to fulfill Jeremiah's prophecy, "for I will turn their mourning into joy and will comfort them and give them joy for their sorrow."[99]

A significant aspect of this day is that the birth of the Messiah is predicted to occur on Tisha B'Av. It means that we come from a tradition that, no matter how much hardship, loss, and trauma have occurred, hope, faith, renewal, and goodness are at its core. After any fracture or any death there is a choice to be made. In Deuteronomy, Moses makes an eloquent speech to the children of Israel,[100] telling them to "choose life so that you and your children will live."

When I have been in the depths of mourning and not known how to take the next step forward, I have taken that step by doing a mitzvah, and dedicating it to the loved one I am mourning. One foot in front of the other, one mitzvah after another. In one of my most treasured books, *A Time to Heal: The Lubavitcher Rebbe's Response to Loss and Tragedy*, the Rebbe said, "The way to combat incomprehensible loss and destruction is to counter it with behavior that is similarly incomprehensible—with irrational goodness."[101]

Telling us that the Messiah will be born on Tisha B'Av lights a fire under us. It reminds us that even when we don't know what to do next, even in despair, or in turmoil, there is always a mitzvah to be done, someone to help, always a call to heed.

Just as on Lag B'Omer, when we recall the great teachings of Rashbi on the anniversary of his death, we recall all that the Temple stood for on the anniversary of its destruction. We remember it was the place where the One came to rest. In so remembering, we remember that we, too, are a temple, and make ourselves into the best receptacle to hold and share the light of the Divine.

99 Jeremiah 31:13
100 Deuteronomy 30:19
101 *A Time to Heal: The Lubavitcher Rebbe's Response to Loss and Tragedy*, by Rabbi Mendel Kalmenson, p. 123.

From the Cook

Tisha B'Av is a fasting day. I offer one recipe that not only helps break the fast but also honors the summertime harvest with its mixed fruit topping. Rice dishes are often associated with the breaking of the fast.

206 Molded Caramelized Rice Pudding with Blueberries, Peaches, and Raspberries

Lentils are considered "mourners' food" and are consumed—without added ingredients—before the fast begins.

Molded Caramelized Rice Pudding *with Blueberries, Peaches, and Raspberries*

SERVES 10 TO 12

PUDDING

1¼ cups white long-grain rice

1 quart whole milk

¼ cup sugar

One 2-inch cinnamon stick

5 large egg yolks

2 cups heavy cream

1 teaspoon vanilla extract

CARAMEL

1 cup sugar

½ cup water

TOPPING

¼ cup freshly squeezed
   orange juice

2 tablespoons sugar

1 pint raspberries

1 pint blueberries

3 freestone peaches, stones
   removed, cut into sixths

The recipe is a personal ode to two favorite desserts: rice pudding and crème caramel. It took more than a few tries to get this right. Choosing the right rice was the final answer, one that could absorb the milk and cream to make a tender pudding, but not the caramel, which made the difference. The result is a dessert that delights with its texture and flavor, and beautiful presentation. I made one as part of a dessert selection for friend's birthday when an embarrassment of colorful, local fruit was available for the topping: apricots, sweet cherries, and blueberries. Truth be told, you can make this year-round, using seasonal fruits as toppings: stewed apples and pears, citrus salad, caramelized pineapple, and all those berries that you've kept in the freezer for just this occasion.

All parts of this recipe can be made the day before your fast begins. It just needs to be assembled when you're ready to break the fast.

1. Prior to cooking the pudding, soak the rice in cold water for about an hour.

2. Make the caramel: Combine the sugar with the water in a small saucepan. Bring to a boil, stirring with a silicone spatula and washing down the sides of the pan once or twice with a wet pastry brush—silicone, too, if possible. Cook the syrup until amber-colored (I like dark amber). Immediately remove from the heat and pour into a 2-quart charlotte mold. Repeatedly tilt the mold from side to side in a circular motion until the sides and bottom are evenly coated. Set aside.

3. Make the pudding: Combine the milk, ¼ cup of the sugar, and cinnamon stick in a nonreactive saucepan over medium-low heat and stir to dissolve the sugar. Drain the rice and add to the milk. Cook at a simmer, stirring from time to time to ensure that the rice doesn't stick to the bottom, until the rice is tender, 35 to 40 minutes.

4. While the rice is cooking, whisk together the egg yolks, cream, and vanilla in a bowl.

5. Heat the oven to 350°F.

6. Remove the cooked rice from the heat. Remove the cinnamon stick and add the egg mixture, little by little, to temper the rice and not curdle the eggs. Stir to thoroughly combine.

7. Pour the rice mixture into the prepared mold.

8. Set the mold in a deep roasting pan and fill one-third of the way up the sides with boiling water. Place in the oven and bake until a tester inserted in the center comes out clean—1 hour 15 minutes to 2 hours. Transfer the mold to a wire rack and let cool. Cover with plastic wrap and refrigerate for up to 4 hours or, preferably, overnight.

9. A few hours before serving, make the topping: Combine the orange juice and sugar in a large, nonreactive saucepan over medium heat. When the sugar dissolves, add the raspberries, blueberries, and peaches. Cook until the peaches are tender, 5 to 12 minutes, depending on the ripeness of the peaches. Let cool.

10. To serve, run a knife around the edge of the mold and invert onto a platter. Pour the fruit over the top. Serve immediately.

CHAPTER FOURTEEN

Tu B'Av

This moon's fullness
illuminates the sky
paving the way for our beloved
who awaits us in the field.

From the Rabbi

Susan: *I'd like to hear about the religious significance of this holiday.*
Zoe: There is much beneath the surface when exploring Tu B'Av. Let's begin with the name. Tu B'Av translates as the 15th of the Hebrew month of Av. Tu B'Av, falling on the 15th when the moon's essence is most revealed, is a full-moon holiday like Tu B'Shevat and Purim and the festivals of Sukkot and Pesach. It is striking to note that this holiday follows closely on the heels of Tisha B'Av, the ninth of Av, and offers an uplifting, hopeful, and rewarding final punctuation to our calendar year.

Our last holiday of Tisha B'Av, considered the saddest day on our calendar, carries within it the image of the daughter of Zion who sits upon the ground in mourning.[102] As the painful description continues, Lamentations asks, "O virgin daughter of Zion, your ruin is great like the sea. Who can heal you?"[103] The rabbis teach that within Tu B'Av, there is a healing for Tisha B'Av. I believe that within this almost unnoticed day, outside of Israel, there is a message essential to complement, balance, and heal our entire yearly cycle. The Mishnah[104] says that there were no days as joyous as Tu B'Av and Yom Kippur. Here, we focus on Tu B'Av, the holiday that arrives in late summer and at the beginning of the grape harvest.

On this night in ancient times, the "daughters of Jerusalem," the unmarried

---

102 Lamentations 2:10
103 Lamentations 2:13
104 Ta'anit 4:9

young women, went out into the vineyards and danced. They wore borrowed white dresses so as not to embarrass anyone who didn't have their own. Waiting for them, also dressed in white, were the young unmarried men. The women called out saying, "Young man! Lift up your eyes and see what you are choosing! Don't pay attention to beauty, but rather, look at the family..."

It is important to note that within these few lines, there contains so much essence of core Jewish values. We are taught that not embarrassing someone is of the utmost importance and that one should never be singled out for how poor or wealthy they are. This is so important that it even extends beyond life. Reading the description of the borrowed white dresses, I'm reminded of our custom to be buried in a plain white inexpensive linen shroud. It was Rabbi Gamliel the Elder,[105] from the early first century, who asked to be buried this way and began the tradition we still follow today. In his day, the wealthy buried their loved ones in expensive shrouds. Concerned for the well-being of people who could not afford such things, he strove to level the playing field and modeled returning to the earth in a simple manner that was attainable for everyone. It is also our Jewish custom in this country to be buried in a plain pine box. We do this partly so that we go back to the earth as quickly as possible, and also that there is no disparity between those who have and those who do not have.

These rituals and ideas are the crucial core values that affirm we are all created B'tzelem Elohim, in the image of God and we guard one another's dignity. It's important to note that the young women in our Tu B'Av story were quick to point out that physical beauty was not to be the focal point; instead, they stressed that the young men should look to the family for their goodness.

The possibility of finding a partner for those who wanted one is reason enough to understand the joy of Tu B'Av, but the Mishnah cites several other reasons to be joyous as well. The one I want to explore circles back to Tisha B'Av and the story of the spies. As we recall from the previous chapter, God had promised the land to the Israelites, the one flowing with milk and honey. After exploring the land for themselves, most of the spies returned in abject fear, which spread rapidly throughout the community. Instead of having faith in what they had already been told that the Creator would provide protection in that land, the majority of people longed to flee and return to Egypt where they had been slaves. A 40-year decree was set in motion,[106] continuing an unending string of tragedies that began on Tisha B'Av.

If you can bear to imagine this scene, each year on Tisha B'Av, people would dig their own grave and lie in it. Every year, for 39 years, they did this, and each

105   Talmud, Moed Katan 27b
106   Rashi on Taanit 30b 12:1

time, deaths tragically occurred. The next morning, those who had "the soul of life" would rise out of their grave and continue their journey. In the 40th year, people once again dug their grave on Tisha B'Av, and the next morning, everyone miraculously discovered that no one had died. Thinking that perhaps they had miscalculated the date, they continued this each night until the full moon, on Tu B'Av, when they realized they had in fact been correct in their calculations and still no one had died. They understood the decree had finally been completed. In gratitude, they established Tu B'Av as a Yom Tov.[107]

Whatever we may think of this story of extreme proportions, it carries within it a message of renewal. Our collective psyches travel from the mourning daughter of Zion in Tisha B'Av to the dancing daughters of Jerusalem. We have gone from destruction and death to beginning a new life in joy. May it be so.

Are there any kinds of observances on this day?

As the days are getting shorter and the nights longer, it is a tradition to increase Torah study in the evening, beginning on this day. It is also the time where we turn our attention inward and begin preparing for Yamim Nora'im (Days of Awe), the High Holy Days. This means it is the perfect opportunity to determine who we might need to reach out to and make amends with. There are only 45 days until Rosh HaShanah, so there is no time to waste in getting this process started. This is after all, a holiday of love, and what could be more loving than making peace wherever it is needed. Like Lag B'Omer, this is a very popular day for weddings as it is considered auspicious to be married on this day.

As we have seen with other holidays, the way our ancestors marked and celebrated their holidays was forever changed or abandoned after the destruction of the Temple and so it was for Tu B'Av. It was not until recent decades in Israel that this holiday received an infusion of attention and the added name of Chag HaAhavah (Festival of Love.)

Rabbi Hillel encouraged his students to "be among the disciples of Aaron, loving peace, perusing peace, loving people and drawing them close to Torah."[108] I can't think of a better way to celebrate Tu B'Av than taking on a mitzvah to help in the spread of peace.

Ketivah v'Chatima Tovah (May you be Inscribed
and Sealed in the Book of Life).

---

107   Literally "a good day," but a term reserved for holidays
108   Mishnah, Pirkei Avot 1:12

From the Cook

My Jewish Israeli friends who are mostly secular talk about Tu B'Av—the Festival of Love—as being popular in their native country, and particularly celebrated in kibbutzim where the kibbutzniks are almost always secular. Festivities include dressing in white clothes, dancing, singing, eating delicious food, and finding love. I think it's a perfect time to dress up in your summertime whites (always a good choice) and make food with the wealth of the ongoing harvest of tender and highly flavored produce from watermelons to nectarines—and everything in between—then feast, dance, and sing until you fall in love for the first time. Or all over again.

Watermelon Salad, Pickled Cherry Tomatoes, Feta, Black Olives

SERVES 6

TOMATOES

1 cup apple cider vinegar

1 cup water

1 tablespoon flaky sea salt

1 tablespoon sugar

Peeled strips of zest from 1 lemon

2 tablespoons fresh mint leaves, plus more for garnish (optional)

Pinch of Aleppo pepper flakes

1 pint assorted cherry tomatoes

SALAD

3 pounds seedless watermelon, scooped into 1-inch balls or cut into chunks (3 to 4 cups)

¼ cup extra-virgin olive oil

¼ cup coarsely chopped cured Moroccan olives

½ cup crumbled feta

Watermelon salads are frequent summertime salad options. This one gives a nod to the Eastern European custom of pickling melon by pickling the tomatoes instead. I use mint instead of the usual dill and add not only feta for saltiness, but also Moroccan black olives as a way of highlighting the other ingredients. For my salad, a kind of Pantone color chart of reds, I scoop out melon balls to imitate the cherry tomato shape.

1. Combine the vinegar, water, salt, sugar, lemon zest, mint leaves, and Aleppo pepper flakes in a large jar with a lid. Shake to incorporate the ingredients.

2. Use a toothpick to prick a few holes in each of the cherry tomatoes, then add them to the pickling liquid. Let the tomatoes stand for at least 2 days in a cool, dark place.

3. Make the salad: Place the watermelon balls in a large bowl. Add the olive oil, olives, feta, and drained cherry tomatoes. Toss to combine.

4. Serve right away or later. The salad will keep for up to 2 days, refrigerated, in a covered bowl.

I've been fascinated by pickled watermelons since my first food shopping trip out to Brighton Beach, situated alongside the crashing waves of the Atlantic Ocean, in New York City's borough of Brooklyn. Brighton Beach has a famously Russian Jewish population with more than a few markets—including a couple of huge supermarkets—that sell everything an Eastern European immigrant would desire. Most of the markets keep big barrels of pickled watermelon—whole pieces, not just the rinds, for sale.

Pesce in Saor

SERVES 6 TO 8

½ cup neutral vegetable oil

3 medium onions, sliced thinly (3 to 4 cups)

1 cinnamon stick

2 cups white wine vinegar

¼ cup raisins

2 pounds flounder fillets, rinsed and dried on paper towels

½ cup all-purpose flour

2 teaspoons flaky sea salt

½ cup olive oil

¼ cup pine nuts

Bay leaves (optional)

Optional garnish: tiny-diced Preserved Lemons (page 41)

Pesce in saor, which translates from Venetian dialect as "flavorful fish," was a simple fishermen's dish of fried fish marinated in onions and vinegar. Then, the Mizrahi Jews of the Middle East contributed raisins and pine nuts to the recipe, and the simple dish became even more flavorful. It continues to evolve as simpatico ingredients are added.

There are two options in this recipe: bay leaves tucked under the fillets as they marinate and a garnish of diced preserved lemons, something I like because of the extra punch of salt and citrus that they add.

1. Heat the vegetable oil in a medium skillet over medium heat. Add the sliced onions and cinnamon stick to the hot oil. Lower the heat to low and simmer until the onions are translucent and soft, 30 to 40 minutes. Add the vinegar and raisins and simmer for another 15 minutes.

2. Stir together the flour and salt on a dinner plate.

3. Lightly dredge the fillets with the flour mixture and set aside.

Jews began to settle in Venice in the 13th century when they arrived from the Iberian Peninsula, North Africa, and Germany. The food styles and spices that traveled with them, together with their adherence to kosher dietary law, had a big influence on the Venetian cucina. Famously, the use of almonds in all sorts of sweet pastries, goose fat in risottos, and the addition of pine nuts and raisins to the vinegary fish dishes already made by local fishermen.

4. Heat the olive oil in a large skillet over medium heat. When the oil bubbles, fry the fish until golden on each side, about 2 minutes per side. When cooked, transfer them to a paper towel–lined plate.

5. To assemble: Arrange a layer of fish in the bottom of a 2-quart oval or rectangular baking dish. Cover with the onion mixture. Sprinkle some of the pine nuts over the top. Continue layering the fish, onion mixture, and pine nuts until you finish with a layer of fish and a last drizzle of the onion mixture. If you like, tuck bay leaves under each layer on both sides. Cover with plastic wrap and refrigerate for 48 hours.

6. Serve with a garnish of diced preserved lemons (if using).

7. Leftover fish will keep, refrigerated, for up to 5 days.

Fresh Corn Pancakes
with Nectarines Cooked in Honey

**MAKES APPROXIMATELY
FOURTEEN 2½-INCH
PANCAKES**

PANCAKES

2 cups Bisquick

2 large eggs

1¼ cups buttermilk

1 cup fresh corn kernels
(from about 2 ears)

Unsalted butter for skillet

NECTARINES

2 tablespoons unsalted butter

3 nectarines, skin on, pitted
and sliced into thin wedges

1 tablespoon freshly
squeezed lemon juice

2 tablespoons honey

½ teaspoon ground cinnamon

½ teaspoon pure vanilla
extract

Optional garnish: plain,
Greek-style yogurt, sour
cream, more melted
butter—or if you want to
be completely decadent,
the Raspberry Ice Cream
in the following recipe
(page 217)

Would you believe that corn and nectarines have an affinity for each other when they share a recipe? By adding honey to this late-summer dish, you'll get a jump start on Rosh HaShanah, when it's a traditional ingredient used to auger a happy New Year. Try to use local honey whenever you can, as it'll help you control seasonal allergies—by consuming it, you are reaping the benefits of what local bees have dined on to make it.

Horror of all horrors, I use Bisquick to make these pancakes. I jazz them up by using local eggs and buttermilk to make the batter. You'd never know the difference.

1. Combine the Bisquick, eggs, and buttermilk in a large bowl and stir thoroughly. Add almost all the corn kernels, reserving a handful for garnish.

2. Melt some butter in a large skillet over medium-high heat. Add a little less than ¼ cup of batter to the skillet per cake. When the edges appear golden, flip the cakes and cook them until firm. Remove and keep them warm while cooking the others.

3. Meanwhile, make the nectarines: Place another skillet or shallow pan over medium heat on a nearby burner. Add the butter. When it has melted, add the nectarines and toss to coat them. Cook, stirring occasionally. After about 3 minutes, add the lemon juice, honey, and cinnamon and toss to evenly coat the fruit. Continue to cook until the nectarines are soft but not mushy. Add the vanilla, toss, and remove from the heat.

4. Serve the warm pancakes topped with nectarines and garnished with yogurt, sour cream, more butter, or ice cream—and a sprinkling of fresh corn.

Grilled Peaches Melba
with Raspberry Ice Cream

SERVES 6

ICE CREAM

4 large egg yolks

½ cup plus 1 tablespoon sugar

⅓ cup plus 1 tablespoon Chambord

1 cup whole milk or plant-based milk (I use oat milk)

2 cups heavy cream

½ pint fresh raspberries, smashed with 1 tablespoon sugar and 1 tablespoon Chambord

This is my combined ode to a summer of good ingredients, love, and the classic dessert Peach Melba, created by the French chef Auguste Escoffier to honor the early 20th-century Australian soprano Nellie Melba.

Make the ice cream 8 to 24 hours in advance of serving.

MAKE THE ICE CREAM

1. Whisk together the egg yolks and sugar in a medium bowl until pale and slightly foamy.

2. Gently heat the milk in a small saucepan, taking care not to scorch it. When the milk appears to erupt around the edges, remove from the heat and pour in the ⅓ cup of Chambord. Pour a bit of milk into the egg mixture and stir. Pour the tempered egg mixture into the remaining milk and return the saucepan to low heat. Use a silicone spoon or spatula to stir the mixture up from the bottom until it clings, like a thin custard, to the spoon.

3. Pour the cream into a large bowl and place a fine-mesh sieve over it. Pour the custard through the sieve and combine with the cream.

4. Transfer the mixture to your ice-cream maker—a simple, economical electric mixer will do just fine. Spin until the mixture resembles ice cream. Add the smashed raspberries and spin for another 60 seconds. Transfer the ice cream to quart- and/or pint-size containers, and freeze immediately.

CONTINUES

RASPBERRY SAUCE

1 pint fresh raspberries

1 tablespoon sugar

PEACHES

6 small to medium freestone peaches, cut in half along their seam, pit removed

1 tablespoon freshly squeezed lemon juice

2 tablespoons amaretto liqueur

MAKE THE RASPBERRY SAUCE

1. Add the raspberries and sugar to a food processor and process until smooth, 3 to 4 minutes. Scrape out of the processor into a small bowl. Cover and refrigerate until ready to serve. If the raspberry seeds are annoying to you, you can sieve the sauce into the bowl before refrigerating.

MAKE THE PEACHES

1. Add the peaches to a medium bowl. Toss in the lemon juice and amaretto liqueur and set aside.

2. Fire up a grill or grill pan over high heat. Place the peaches cut side down on the grill and baste the skin with remaining juice from the bowl. Grill until the peaches are a deep golden color. Flip them and continue to grill until they appear to be cooked through (all of this will happen quickly with ripe, in-season peaches, about 2 minutes or so on each side). Remove from the grill and let cool.

TO SERVE

1. Add both sides of each peach, skin side down, side-by-side in individual serving bowls. Place a large scoop of raspberry ice cream into the overlapping cavities of each peach. Cover the ice cream with the raspberry sauce and serve immediately.

Cornmeal Shortcakes
with Passion Fruit Curd and Blackberry and Blueberry Sauce

SERVES 8

BLACKBERRY AND BLUE-BERRY SAUCE (MAKES ABOUT 3 CUPS)

2 pints blueberries, rinsed and picked over

½ pint blackberries

1 tablespoon honey

1 tablespoon freshly squeezed lemon juice

¼ cup cassis or St Germain liqueur

SHORTCAKES

1½ cups all-purpose flour

½ cup yellow cornmeal

4 teaspoons baking powder

3 tablespoons sugar

8 tablespoons (1 stick) cold unsalted butter, cut into pieces

1 large egg, lightly beaten

½ cup buttermilk, plus more for glazing

1 cup Passion Fruit Curd (page 78)

A Tu B'Av celebration needs lots of sweet things to eat. I can't help wanting to turn all the available late-summer produce into delicious choices.

MAKE THE BLACKBERRY AND BLUEBERRY SAUCE

1. Combine the blueberries, blackberries, honey, lemon juice, and liqueur in a large nonreactive saucepan over medium heat. Cook until the blueberries begin to collapse, 10 to 15 minutes.

2. Remove from the heat and let cool.

MAKE THE SHORTCAKES

1. Heat the oven to 450°F.

2. Combine the flour, cornmeal, baking powder, and sugar in a food processor. With the machine running, add the butter, a few pieces at a time, then the egg and buttermilk. Process until all the ingredients are just mixed.

3. Place ⅓-cup portions of the dough about 2 inches apart on an ungreased baking sheet. Use a pastry brush or spoon to coat the tops of the cakes with buttermilk. Bake for 10 to 15 minutes, at most. Check after 10 minutes; the tops should look slightly browned. Remove from the oven and let cool on a wire rack.

4. To serve, split the shortcakes in half. Spread the bottom half with 2 tablespoons of the passion fruit curd and top with berry sauce. Cover with the top half of the shortcake, set slightly askew. Serve right away.

Limonana

MAKES 6 TO 8 DRINKS (BECAUSE YOU MIGHT WANT A SHORT ONE)

1 cup freshly squeezed lemon juice (from 4 to 5 lemons)

½ cup sugar, or more to taste

½ cup packed fresh mint leaves, preferably spearmint

1 cup cold water

4 cups ice cubes

Vodka or bourbon (optional)

I drank a *limonana* for the first time at the late, lamented Dizengoff Street in the Chelsea Market in New York City. A slushy mixture of mint and lemon, the drink went down like a snowdrift and balled up against my stomach with such a start that I gasped, then I couldn't wait for the next sip. The Middle Eastern drink, popular with Israelis—who might pick one up on the real Dizengoff Street in Tel Aviv before heading to a nearby Mediterranean beach—is the perfect cooling-off beverage on a steamy day, or as an accompaniment to a plate of hummus.

1. Combine the lemon juice and sugar in a blender and run the machine on the "puree/smoothie" setting—or something similar—for 30 to 45 seconds to blend.

2. Add the mint and run the machine, at the same setting, for about 45 seconds, to begin to pulverize the mint.

3. Add the cold water and run the machine until mint is completely broken down (you don't want it to catch in your throat).

4. Add the ice, then run the blender on the "grind/crush ice" setting until slushy.

5. Serve right away.

6. Make into a cocktail by adding a shot of vodka or bourbon to each drink.

Acknowledgments

From Susan Simon

To my agent and friend, Charlotte Sheedy, who arrived in my life at just the right time. An author's agent in the truest way, Charlotte stayed with this project, never lagging in enthusiasm for it, until it became what you're reading. To Rabbi Zoe B Zak, who agreed to go on this journey with me shortly after lunch. To my editor, Ann Treistman, who bravely took on and stood behind this unusual but much needed book. To the others at the Countryman Press, who were real cheerleaders: Allison Chi, the book's designer, who understands how well words and color play with each other; Maya Goldfarb, Devorah Backman, and Rhina Garcia, who made sure this book got out to you. To Iris Bass, for her laser-focused editorial comments.

To Roy Finamore, who acquired my first book in 1989, and is now a dear friend who contributed the challah recipe. To Cary Guy, for late nights talks between New York and the Dominican Republic and a stellar preserved lemon recipe. To Michael Harris, for non-stop shipments of the produce that he grows on his California property, especially the divine passion fruit. To Olga Cipolla, *per il suo aiuto con le castagne, i ceci e i carciofi.* To Roselle Chartock, for sharing her book, *The Jewish Life of Elvis Presley.* To David Goldberg, who talked me through Yiddish and Hebrew expressions, and his memories of Jewish holidays. To Margo Johnston, for giving me permission to use her late mother Eden's recipe for applesauce. To Donna Hordes, for her help in all things Israeli, especially her remembrances of the way holidays were celebrated in her native country.

To Sue Decker of Blue Star Farms, who put aside some of her precious sugar snap peas and strawberries before they sold out, because I'm a late-arriver to the Saturday morning Hudson Farmers' Market. To Jen Hewett, who many times helped me through my severe case of technophobia. To photographer David McIntyre, for capturing me in just the right light.

Dearest Bonnie Kovacs, carer of animals and humans, who gifted me with swaths of uninterrupted work time while she took my dog, Bean, out on amazing afternoon adventures.

Thanks very much.

From Zoe B Zak

This book came to life because of many different hands and hearts. Thank you to Susan Simon, for the initial seed of inspiration for this project, and for all the deliciousness you brought to the table. To my agent and friend, the one and only Charlotte Sheedy, who never stopped believing in this book, and whose belief in me buoyed me beyond measure. To Ann Treistman, editorial director at Countryman Press, for your passionate dedication to making this book a reality and for your enthusiasm every step of the way. To the ever-positive Countryman team, Devorah Backman, Allison Chi, Rhina Garcia, and Maya Goldfarb. To Rabbi Michael Goldman, who, with his scholarly eyes, became my trusted fact and reality checker. To Stacey Brooks, who, as always, went beyond the call with towering generosity and edited my final draft. To copy editor Iris Bass, for your fastidious attention to every detail. To my Temple Israel of Catskill family, who, for years with great enthusiasm, has gone along with my every creative approach to the Jewish holidays, and who joyfully cheered me on in writing this book. To all my teachers and rabbis, who have inspired me in countless ways. To Rabbi Yitzhok and Rebbetzin Leah Hecht, Rabbi AB and Rebbetzin Binie Itkin, for modeling everything you teach, and for the immense kindness you share with me and countless others. To Henry Sapoznik, for your steady moral support and wise counsel. To Angela Orli, for your tiny notes of encouragement left in unexpected places, for all your delicious meals, and your help in multifarious ways that gifted me precious time to write. You inspire me every single day.

Index

"In *The Cook and the Rabbi*, Rabbi Zoe B Zak provides clear, meaning-ful explanations of the Jewish Holy Days, while Susan Simon provides new favorite meals to help us build new delicious memories. This book can be the spark for some to learn the meaning of the Holy Days, while enhancing the culinary delight of others to enhance their observance."
—Rabbi Jeff Roth, founder/director of the Awakened Heart Project for Contemplative Judaism